RAILROAD RADIO

HEARING AND UNDERSTANDING
RAILROAD RADIO COMMUNICATIONS & SYSTEMS

by Vincent Reh, WA2AUY

BYRON HILL PUBLISHING COMPANY

GRAND ISLE, VERMONT

P.O. BOX 197
GRAND ISLE, VT 05458
AMERICA

Copyright © 1996 by Vincent Reh

All rights reserved. No part of this book may be reproduced, in any form or means whatsoever, without written permission from the publisher except for brief quotations used in critical reviews.

Printed in the United States of America by The Offset House, Essex, Vt.

Cover design by Greg Giordano, Rhombus Communications, Burlington, Vt.
Cover photo courtesy of Atchison, Topeka & Santa Fe Railway Company
Inside design, illustrations, and photos by Vincent Reh, unless noted otherwise

International Standard Book No. 0-9651599-0-6
Library of Congress Catalogue Card No. 96-96107

Dedicated to the forgotten pioneers of wireless communication

A.C. Brown
Amos Dolbear
Mahlon Loomis
Fr. Joseph Murgas
Willoughby Smith
Nathan Stubblefield
John Trowbridge

On the cover—*Train dispatcher at work, Schaumburg Operations Center, Atchison, Topeka & Santa Fe Railway, Schaumburg, Illinois* (courtesy AT&SF Railway Co.)

ACKNOWLEDGEMENTS

I would like to thank the following individuals and organizations for their assistance and encouragement, without which this book could not have been published. V.R.

Claude Addy, CP Rail System
Margaret T. Anderson, Chesapeake & Ohio Historical Society, Inc.
Julie Brock-Tettenhorst, Tandy Corp.
Gus Bruno, Antenna Specialists Co.
Lee Burbage, Pennsylvania Railroad Technical & Historical Society
Vince Caputo, Andrew Corporation
Fred Childs, W0WQ, Northern Pacific Railway, ret.
Mike Cook, New-Tronics Antenna Corp.
David M. Corney, WB2FCR, friend and consultant
Kevin Cox, N7KTP, Optoelectronics, Inc.
James M. Davis, Conrail Technical Society
Eddie DeFell, Atchison, Topeka & Santa Fe Railway Co.
William F. Dority, consultant, GE-Harris Railway Electronics
Thomas D. Dressler, Norfolk & Western Historical Society, Inc.
W.K. Dunbar, AD9E, Morse Telegraph Club, Inc.
Ronald A. Duncan, Avtec, Inc.
Kermit Geary, Jr., Conrail Historical Society
A.L. George, Safetran Systems Corp.
Bob Grove, WA4PYQ, Grove Enterprises, Inc.
Karin Hagin, Qualcomm, Inc.
Willard A. Harvey, Nickel Plate Historical Society
Donald I. Henry, Shakespeare Co.
Pat Hopkins, General Railway Signal Corp.
John G. King, Affiliation for Baltimore & Ohio System Historical Research
Fred LaRose, Vermont Railway
Larsen Electronics, Inc.
Bryce Lee, *Railpace Newsmagazine*
Robert E. Lowell, Aerotron-Repco Sales, Inc.
MFJ Enterprises, Inc.
Jon B. Main, Pennsylvania Railroad Technical & Historical Society
Larry Marnes, Morse Telegraph Club
C.D. Melzer, Amtech Systems Corp.
H. Warren Middleton, W8CXD, Norfolk & Western Historical Society, Inc.
John T. Nasci, Esq., WA2DOL, friend and consultant
Jack Pelzman, KD6SHN, Yaesu U.S.A.
Phillip O. Ritter, Pennsylvania Railroad Technical & Historical Society
Heather Sinclair, Sinclair Technologies, Inc.
Robert A. Snead, Pulse Electronics, Inc.
Nora M. Songer, Cattron, Inc.
Janice Szabo, Shelburne Museum
Chester H. Wesman, KB7KN, Great Northern Railway Historical Society
Wayne Wilson, WB8TSO, Tandy Corp.
Elaine Zegarski, Theimeg, Inc.

Caveats

When using a scanner to monitor railroad radio communications, as with anything else, common sense and courtesy go a long way. Improper use of a scanner and unsafe actions on your part can at the least make you a nuisance, and at worst, get you arrested or KILLED.

Please note that the author cannot be responsible for the way scanners are used or for any actions resulting from scanner use. The way you use a scanner is entirely up to you and completely your own business. If you choose to ignore the safety warnings and usage recommendations described below and throughout the text, you do so at your own risk.

Scanner Safety

Many safety issues are discussed in the text. It is imperative that you understand them completely and follow them closely.

Be careful with antennas. Outdoor antennas must be properly installed and supported per manufacturer recommendations. Improperly installed antennas can fall, causing property damage, personal injury, or DEATH.

Keep all antennas away from power lines and properly protected from lightning. If you don't, you could be ELECTROCUTED or start a serious fire.

Remember that radio communication is not always a reliable predictor of train activity. Trains can come and go without any radio indication whatsoever. Always be alert and expect a train on any track, in any direction, at any time.

Finally.....STAY OFF AND AWAY FROM TRACKS, even at public grade crossings! Keep in mind that all railroad lands and structures are private property and that you can be arrested for trespassing. Get permission before entering railroad property.

REMEMBER! *THE SCANNER THAT PROMPTED YOU TO CROSS THE TRACKS UNSAFELY WON'T BE ANY GOOD IF YOU'RE NOT AROUND TO USE IT.*

Scanner Etiquette

Please remember to be courteous when using a scanner in public areas or around railfans with video cameras or tape recorders. Turn off your scanner or use headphones.

Don't use your scanner to be the first on the scene at accidents or other incidents unless you are qualified to do so. Otherwise, you'll just get in the way and further irritate public safety and railroad agents, especially if they see you with a scanner.

Be discreet—don't repeat anything you hear that could prove to be embarrassing to you or anyone else. Besides violating federal regulations on divulging information, you could help perpetuate the myth that all scanner listeners are voyeuristic technocreeps plying their trade with exotic hacking gear.

Trademark Notices

Private Line, Tone Private Line, Digital Private Line, TPL, DPL, and Handie-Talkie are trademarks of Motorola, Inc. Touch-Tone is a trademark of American Telephone & Telegraph Co.

Table of Contents

1 Introduction
    The Canadian-American rail network 1
    Need for radio communications 2
    Pre-radio operations: schedules and train orders 2
    Development of inductive communications 6
    Pennsylvania Railroad "Trainphone" 8
    Development of radio communications 11
    Post-war VHF radio boom 12
    Radio spectrum and frequencies 17
    Transmission characteristics 18

2 Modern Railroad Radio Communication Systems
    Dispatching centers 21
    Base stations 23
    Passive repeaters 26
    Active repeaters 26
    Coded squelch 29
    Mobile radios 30
    Communication links 31
    Portable radios 37
    Remote receivers 38
    End-of-train devices 41
    Radio alarm detectors 43
    Cellular telephones 46
    Private branch exchanges 46
    Radiotelemetric links 48
    Global positioning systems 50
    Automatic equipment identification 51
    Radio remote control 53

3 Radio Operations
    Dispatchers 57
    Train crews 57
    Yards 58
    Maintenance 61
    Police 63
    Taxis 64
    Transmitter identification 64

4 Scanners and Monitoring
    What is a scanner? 65
    What can be heard? 66
    Is it illegal to use a scanner? 66
    Railfanning with a scanner 68
    Advance warning of approaching trains 68
    Determining what kind of train is approaching 70
    Understanding railroad operations 71
    Buying a scanner 72
    Scanner configurations 74
    Performance considerations 77
    Operating frequencies 81
    Power sources 85

5 Improving Scanner Performance
    Antennas 90
    Feedline 102
    Signal amplifiers 105
    Professional radio equipment 109
    Ham radio gear 110
    Computer interfaces 110
    Coded squelch decoders 112
    Voice-activated recorders 113
    External speakers and audio amplifiers 114
    Area repeaters 116

Beam antennas 117
Towers 119
Passive repeaters 120

6 Scanning on a Budget
Used equipment 121
Buying used gear 122
The market 123
Homebrewing 129

7 The Future of Railroad Radio Communications
Spectrum congestion 139
Trunked radio systems 140
Automatic train control 141
Listening in 142

A Selected Railroad Radio Frequencies • 145

B AAR Channel Designators • 149

C Coded Squelch Tone Frequencies • 151

D Reporting Marks for Selected Railroads • 153

E Sample Train Symbols • 157

F Rules Governing Radio Use • 159

G Information Sources • 167

H Glossary of Terms • 169

Index • 193

CHAPTER 1

Introduction

At 240,000 route miles, the railroad network in the United States and Canada is immense. Hundreds of commercial and industrial railroads haul and deliver a remarkable variety of commodities, everything from fruits and vegetables in Southern California to iron ore in Labrador. In 1992 alone, railroads moved over 1.13 trillion ton-miles of freight.

In spite our love affair with automobiles and air travel, passengers make over three billion trips by rail every year, from coast to coast, across town, and all points in between. In 1992, U.S. railroads racked up a total of 14 billion passenger miles in addition to freight mileage.

It goes without saying that running and coordinating all this traffic is not a simple task—railroads employ over 300,000 people to keep freight and passengers on the move. Trains must be carefully dispatched and routed to avoid conflicts and delays, and at the worst, collisions and accidents, and locomotives, cars, signals, communication facilities, and the tracks themselves must be carefully guarded, inspected, and maintained to avoid problems and costly failures.

The ability to effectively manage and coordinate any organization depends upon the quantity and quality of information available to all its participants, and railroads are no exception. This is especially true due to the diverse, far-flung, and highly mobile nature of railroad operations. To keep in touch with their employees, railroads make extensive use of telephone and radio communication networks.

While telephones may seem to be the obvious solution for desk-bound employees, the situation is markedly different for employees on the move. How does one effectively communicate with a train rolling down the main line at 79 mph or a track inspector working in remote areas without a telephone in sight? And what if someone needed to communicate with both at the same time? How can a caboose communicate the position of a train to its locomotive? Although lineside and cab signals provide valuable operating information to train crews, there is only one truly effective solution: Two-way radio.

Development of Railroad Radio Communications

As more and more trains found their way onto the burgeoning rail network in the late nineteenth century, the need for more effective communications became patently clear. With too many trains and not enough track, collisions and wrecks were inevitable.

Running trains on fixed schedules—i.e., wait at siding X for trains A, B, and C to pass before continuing down the line—took a giant step towards resolving the problem, but left plenty of room for mistakes and errors in judgement, often with deadly results. Even when things did work out, trains often wasted time waiting for other trains to pass, some of which were delayed or cancelled by track conditions, mechanical failures, accidents, and miscommunication.

To help overcome these problems, railroads implemented train order operations to govern train movements over certain segments, or blocks, of the railroad. Trains needed permission from the dispatcher—the person responsible for coordinating all train movements under the authority of a division superintendent—to enter or occupy a block. Once inside a block, all movements were governed by train orders that regulated such things as train speed, track occupation, and passage to the next block.

To coordinate train movements, the dispatcher relied upon train location reports telegraphed to him by a network of operators situated in stations along the tracks. By knowing the locations of trains, the dispatcher could route trains with maximum efficiency. Since trains could not enter a block without the permission of the division superintendent, the chances of wrecks and collisions were greatly reduced.

In addition to sending train status information to the dispatcher, operators were also responsible for relaying orders to trains. To minimize delays, operators would set lineside signals called order boards to indicate whether orders were to be picked up, and if so, whether or not trains had to stop to collect them. Whenever possible, operators would "hoop up" orders to moving trains. Normally, trains were stopped only when congestion or other problems prevented safe occupation of the next block. If no orders were to be picked up, trains would travel straight through.

When train crews needed to contact the dispatcher or operator, e.g., to communicate a mechanical or personal problem, they would simply tie a note to an unlit fusee and drop it on the platform for pickup by the operator. Since operators were required to inspect all passing trains for signs of trouble, these messages were rarely missed.

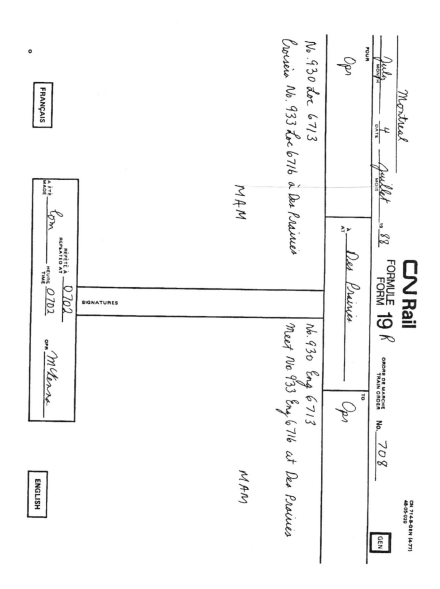

Form 19 train order. Form 19s were typically "hooped up" to train crews on the fly, however, this particular order was given via radio as denoted by the "R." The order authorized Train 930 to operate over Canadian National's Montréal–Deux-Montagnes electrified commuter line. The locomotives named, 6713 & 6716, were recently retired after more than 70 years of continuous service.

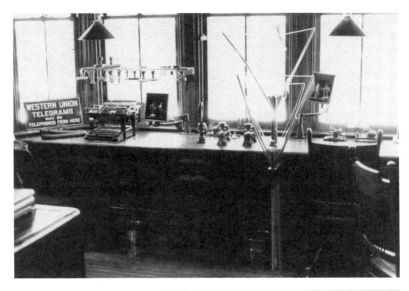

Top: *Bay window of a train station showing (l–r) typewriter or "mill," telegraph sounder, ticket validators and code key, order hoops with attached orders, sounder, spare sounder, and telegraph relay.* Bottom: *Operator's desk showing (l–r) spare sounders, code key, jackbox for circuit selection, lightning arrestor, sounder [above arrestor], and partial view of a copy press.* (Both photos courtesy Shelburne Museum)

Operators were so named because they were responsible for operating telegraph equipment as well as track switches and signals to route trains into and out of sidings or other lines as directed by the dispatcher. These tasks were performed in conjunction with other responsibilities.

Although train orders and operators increased operating efficiency, the system contained serious shortcomings. Telegraph lines were often damaged by storms, resulting in a loss of communications. Even in the best of circumstances, the operator served merely as an intermediary, acting as an information relay between the dispatcher and the train crew. This limited the efficiency of the dispatching process and increased the probability of incorrect information being given to trains.

If serious problems developed over the road, conductors were forced to either climb lineside poles to connect their telegraph keys or phone sets, or walk to the nearest telephone callbox to contact dispatchers about the delay. To keep trains from colliding, flagmen would "hit the cinders" and walk back a mile or so from the caboose to flag approaching trains. In short, over-the-road problems played havoc with schedules, caused unnecessary delays, and created safety hazards.

Although the solution was clear—direct communication between train crews and operators/dispatchers—implementing the solution was another story. As far back as 1838, systems were envisioned that would sound alarms in locomotives if trains were on a collision course, but the wireless technology needed to implement the ideas simply didn't exist. A little more than 40 years would pass before the first wireless train communication system was installed.

In 1881, A.C. Brown, an officer with the Eastern Telegraph Company of England, implemented the first wireless train communication system. Brown's system was based on induction telephony, a non-radio technique that used electromagnetic coupling, or transformer action, to send and receive voice messages over standard telephone apparatus.

In Brown's system, an insulated wire was coiled around the locomotive and a battery connected to one end of the line and a telephone set to the other. The battery and telephone were interconnected to complete the loop. Another wire was strung along the tracks on insulators, one end of which went to ground and the other to a battery and telephone set. One side of the telephone set was grounded to complete the loop.

The electromagnetic force produced by one loop would transmit, or induce, a weak electrical current into the other. By talking into the telephone, it was possible to vary the amount of induced current. These current variations were then picked up by the receiver and converted into speech, thus allowing train crews and operators to speak with each other.

In 1883, another Englishman, Willoughby Smith, implemented an induction-based signalling system that consisted of a series of coils buried beneath the tracks and a pickup coil attached to the bottom of locomotives. To signal a train, various tones were modulated onto the track coils for pickup by passing trains. To transmit orders to the train, each command (approach, stop, etc.) was assigned a distinct tone.

By 1885, Thomas Edison became aware of the on-going experiments with inductive communications. With the assistance of Smith, Edison installed experimental inductive telegraph systems at Staten Island, N.Y. and on the Milwaukee Road. In 1887, Edison installed a working system on the Lehigh Valley between Perth Junction, N.J. and Easton, Pa. On October 6th, the first day of operation, over 400 telegraph messages were handled between the train and stations around the national telegraph network. Because the system used an inductive link and existing telegraph lines, it was called a "wired-wireless" system.

Despite the success of this installation, Edison's system did not initially take off, perhaps owing to indifference or the expense of implementing the system on a larger scale. However, by the twenties, the value of inductive communications was becoming apparent to some roads. In 1920, the New York Central, in conjunction with the DeForest Wireless Company, installed and demonstrated a working induction telegraph system. In 1928, the Pennsylvania demonstrated a Westinghouse system that included voice communication capabilities.

In the thirties, the Pennsylvania developed and refined an inductive "Trainphone" communication system in cahoots with General Electric and Union Switch & Signal. US&S also installed a similar system on the Bessemer & Lake Erie with encouraging results.

During World War II, the Pennsylvania continued to expand and improve its Trainphone system and technology, partly because very high frequency (VHF) radio technologies were restricted to military use. The Pennsy replaced interference-prone amplitude modulation with new frequency modulation techniques. Voice signals were frequency-modulated onto two carrier frequencies—80 and 144 kilohertz (kHz)—to provide dual-channel capability. The low carrier was used for inter/intratrain communications, and the high for communication with lineside operators.

US&S and other suppliers, including General Railway Signal and Aviation Accessories, also supplied induction systems to railroads during the war. The Atlantic Coast Line installed a

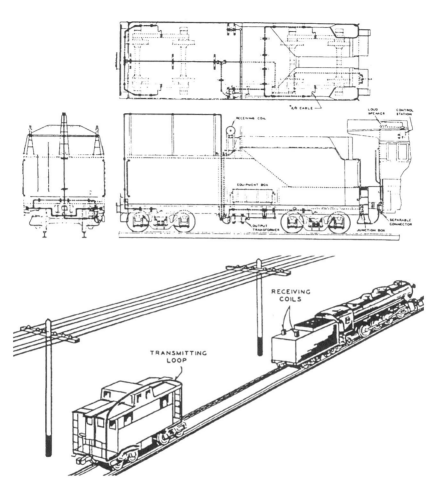

Top: *Pennsylvania Railroad drawing depicting Trainphone components on a steam locomotive tender. The equipment box housed modular, shock-mounted transmitters, receivers, and dynamotor power supply. The cab components included an overhead speaker and an equipment control box, which included a telephone-style handset, volume control, and channel selector. The transmitting loop (in bold) consisted of 1-5/16" copper-clad steel handrail pipe and was coupled to the rails via the trucks and 2/0 flexible cable. A small receiving loop assembly was used for each carrier frequency.* Bottom: *Signals were inductively coupled via the rails and pole-mounted lines. The rails themselves were used to complete the loop on cabooses and tenders. Diesel locomotives used single-ended (non-loop) handrails for both transmit and receive. Wayside stations were wired to the pole lines.* (Railroad Museum of Pa. / Pa. Historical & Museum Commission; courtesy PRR Technical & Historical Society)

Top: *View of Norfolk & Western class S1A steam locomotive tender showing inductive radio set (topside of tender above "AND") and antenna cabling.* (Thomas Dressler, courtesy N&W Historical Society). Bottom: *View of N&W class S1 steam locomotive showing radio set (topside of tender), antenna cabling, and antenna (the handrail attached to the sides of the boiler jacket). Antennas consisted of copper-coated steel pipe covered with rubber insulation, thus allowing antennas to double as handrails. Connections to an in-cab control box were made through a separate cable.* (Willard A. Harvey)

system following a disastrous late 1943 wreck in which the *East Coast Champion* slammed into a derailed *West Coast Champion*. In addition, the Milwaukee Road, New York Central, Kansas City Southern, Jersey Central, Baltimore & Ohio, Chesapeake & Ohio, and Norfolk & Western implemented or expanded induction systems.

After the war, the VHF radio technology used by the Allies was made available to the private sector. Railroads quickly adopted the new technology at the expense of their induction systems. The Pennsy, on the other hand, continued to rely upon and expand its Trainphone network, and even introduced the Carryphone, a "portable" induction set for brakemen and car inspectors. The 26 lb. unit came complete with batteries, a 30-inch diameter loop, and a shoulder carry strap.

However, by the sixties, the advantages of radio—increased range, portability, reliability, flexibility, interoperability, and ease of installation, especially in automobiles—could no longer be ignored. By the mid-sixties, the Pennsy had installed VHF radios in most of its equipment and offices. In 1967, the new radio system was cut in and the Trainphone system was decommissioned.

Although induction systems have for the most part been supplanted by radio, induction is still used in niche applications where radio isn't usable or feasible, such as in subways. For example, induction is used for signalling and train control on BC Transit's SkyTrain in Vancouver and on the Municipal Railway in San Francisco.

Despite the popularity of induction systems, railroads experimented with radio from its commercial debut in the early part of the century. In 1910, the Union Pacific's Omaha, Neb. headquarters installed a one-way system to telegraph switching information to yard crews. The Lackawanna, working in conjunction with the Marconi Wireless Company, installed the world's first two-way system in 1913. Base stations were established in New York, Scranton, and Binghamton to transmit telegraph and voice signals to trains along the main line. The Binghamton radio tower stands to this day, adjacent to the railroad station.

In the twenties, railroads adopted radio communication technologies from a myriad of suppliers including Westinghouse, Marconi, DeForest, Western Electric, General Electric, RCA, and Zenith. Along with the Union Pacific and the Lackawanna, other roads using radio technologies included the Pennsylvania, the New York Central, and Canadian National.

When the Burlington's stainless-steel *Zephyr*—the world's first diesel-powered trainset—made its famous Denver-to-Chicago run in 1934, radio was used to maintain constant telegraph contact with the train. Despite the success of the run, government regulation and unsuitable technology slowed the progress of radio throughout the thirties and forties.

Many railroads, such as the Pennsy, moved away from radio and began to embrace induction technology. However, with the end of the war and the release of the wartime VHF technology, which was technically superior to induction, radio use experienced a boom on the railroads. Nearly every road that could afford to install VHF equipment did so—in trains, vehicles, and at operations centers. The first VHF system was installed by the Baltimore & Ohio in 1946 to help speed car classification at its New Castle, Pa. yard.

The Gulf, Mobile & Ohio first installed VHF radios in 1947 in yard offices and on locomotives and cabooses used in time-sensitive freights. Because radios were installed in limited numbers, "radio cabooses" were coupled ahead of regular cabooses, making it necessary for crews to walk between the two to use the radio (this was during the pre-pool era when cabooses were permanently assigned to specific crews).

The Great Northern's first regular VHF installation was in 1952 on Minnesota Iron Range trains running to and from the Lake Superior ore docks. The Burlington first tested radios on freights in 1944 at Clyde, Ill., by sending signals between a diesel locomotive and a caboose.

In 1947, the Northern Pacific installed Bendix VHF radio gear in a diesel locomotive and set up a base station at St. Paul. This was followed up by installing more Bendix gear in six diesel switchers at Seattle. In 1949, twenty-three cabooses were Bendix-equipped at Auburn and Yakima. The Erie first installed its so-called "four-way radio-telephone" on 347 miles of its main line in late 1948 *(see page 144)*.

In addition to voice systems, railroads began to experiment with radio remote control technology for locomotives and trains, especially in industrial and yard applications. In 1956, the Norfolk & Western placed a small, battery-powered, remote-controlled locomotive into hump service at its East Portsmouth, Ohio yard.

"Nellybelle," as she was referred to by yard workers, would be dispatched to quickly clear or "trim" cars that did not roll down the hump fast enough to reach their proper yard tracks. Before Nellybelle, a switch engine would be called in, bringing hump operations to a halt. Unfortunately, Nellybelle was damaged in a collision in 1966 and was later scrapped.

Radio was also used to temporarily bridge trackside open wire lines that were damaged by storms. Temporary stations, typically manned by ham radio operators, would relay voice and telegraph messages between disconnected stations via high frequency (HF), shortwave radio. The hams made it possible to keep trains rolling while repairs were made to the telegraph lines.

In the beginning, many railroad employees didn't accept their new radios. Crewmen would grow weary of the chatter and turn their radios off, claiming that equipment had failed or that signals were unreadable. Others proclaimed radio to be a "sissy" innovation and simply refused to use it.

Dispatchers found radio to be both a curse and a blessing. Although radio made for smoother operations, it also increased the amount and density of messages—and stress—they had to handle. Just about everyone on the railroad called the dispatcher to relay messages, order materials, etc. Also, train location information formerly provided by operators was now managed by dispatchers. And, as always, the possibility for miscommunication continued to exist.

Unions were concerned that radio would eliminate jobs and believed that radio operation crossed craft lines. Many train and enginemen believed they were doing operator's work and argued that only members of the Order of Railroad Telegraphers should operate radios. Even Nellybelle raised the ire of the brotherhoods, who didn't like the idea of unmanned locomotive operation. However, when the convenience and safety of radio operations became clear, union resistance waned.

Management either mandated radio use and revised their rulebooks to govern its operation, or simply installed radios and let crews use them as they saw fit, provided they did not violate any existing operating rules. Even today, radio is used only to augment operations; the book of rules is still the ultimate authority *(see Appendix F)*.

Typically, crews had to qualify on radio operations (and still do) by passing an examination covering general radio use. Crews also continue to perform radio checks to make sure their units are functioning properly, much like the mandatory brake test.

As radio use became accepted, railroads developed their own communication styles based on existing operations, new rules, and the personalities of its users. W.K. Dunbar, Morse Telegraph Club president and former telegrapher and dispatcher on the Alton/GM&O relates, "The flagman of one of our freight crews, instead of telling his engineer verbally that the train had cleared the turnouts at Godfrey [Ill.], would hold the handset out the window of the cupola. When the engineer heard the crossing signal bells (in Doppler, yet) he knew he could 'widen on it' and resume maximum authorized speed."

Dunbar continues, "A variation on this was to click the handset button twice, making the resulting squelch tails an imitation of whistle signal 14-B (release brakes-proceed). Even this was too much for one brakeman, who would pick up the handset and say, 'Click-click,' thereby saving 50 percent of the finger labor involved."

Up to the late fifties, most radio equipment relied on "hollow state" technology, i.e., vacuum tube designs. In the mid-fifties, railroads installed the first hybrid systems, or solid state (transistorized) power supplies working with tube transmitters and receivers. Solid state receivers were introduced in the mid-sixties, and totally solid state units were available by the end of the decade. In the ensuing years, increased miniaturization became the goal for radio manufacturers and railroads.

Initially, mobile radios were installed in three parts. A control head containing audio circuitry, a volume control, squelch control (for automatic receiver quieting), channel selector, and handset or speaker was mounted in the locomotive cab, vehicle dash, or at the conductor's desk or cupola in a caboose.

A shock-mounted main radio chassis containing the transmitting and receive circuitry was installed in the nose of diesel locomotives, in weathertight compartments on tender decks or below the cabs in steamers, in the trunk or behind the seat in cars and trucks, and below the bunks in cabooses.

The power supply unit was usually mounted nearby. In locomotives and vehicles, it typically consisted of a motor–generator or mechanical vibrator–converter powered by the auxiliary generator or vehicle electrical system. Later versions used solid state converters. In cabooses, an axle-driven generator charged a battery bank that in turn powered the radio.

Portable units required a hefty battery supply to power the vacuum tubes and were therefore bulky and quite heavy, requiring the use of backpacks or shoulder harnesses.

As solid state electronics, integrated circuits, and batteries became smaller and more sophisticated in the late sixties and throughout the seventies, all-in-one mobile units and hand-held portables became the norm. For the first time, entire radios could be mounted in locomotive cabs and dashboards, and portables could be easily carried in one hand.

By the eighties, increased miniaturization and the use of advanced microprocessor technology allowed manufacturers to pack an impressive array of features into ever-shrinking packages—such things as channel scanning, programmable transmit and receive frequencies, automatic unit identification, and digital control for channel and system access.

Today, U.S. and Canadian railroads of all types and sizes employ the latest radio technology to pass a variety of voice and data communications. The availability of quality, reasonably priced radio gear has made it possible for even the smallest shortline, industrial, or tourist railroad to integrate radio into their operations. In addition to voice traffic, radio is used to transmit telemetry for train control, tracking, signalling, and locomotive and car operating status.

As railroads embrace new radio communication technology, hand and whistle signals, lineside telephones, order hoops, and racks of open wire line are either gone or disappearing at a rapid rate. In North America, these practices remain in use only in Mexico. Old-time telephone and telegraph suppliers—names like Automatic Electric, Stromberg Carlson, and Vibroplex—have been replaced by the likes of Aerotron, Motorola, General Electric, and Harris.

Radio Frequencies and Transmission

Nearly all North American railroads continue to use VHF for their radio communications. VHF covers the frequency range of 30 to 300 megahertz (MHz), formerly known as megacycles (Mc). Railroads use a small segment or "band" of VHF frequencies (also called channels) among FM radio broadcasts and police, marine, fire, taxi, and other transmissions.

In the U.S., most railroads operate their main voice communication networks in a band covering 160.215–161.565 MHz. Canadian roads are also authorized to operate from 159.810–160.200 MHz. In addition, a few railroads (mostly transit) use a limited number of frequencies in the UHF (ultra high frequency) band—typically around 453, 473, 479, and 485 MHz.

Radiotelemetry (coded data) is also transmitted using UHF, typically around 402–470, 806–868, 902–927, and 2,400–2,484 MHz, although 161.115 and 72–76 MHz VHF is also used. For major facility-to-facility links, microwave transmissions are used in the super high frequency (SHF) region from 4,000–11,000 MHz, which is the same as 4–11 gigahertz (GHz).

In addition to standard frequency assignments, a very few tourist, museum, and shortline railroads communicate using citizen's band (CB) and general mobile radio service (GMRS) radios operating in the largely unregulated 27 and 462/467 MHz bands, respectively.

The Federal Communications Commission (FCC) in the U.S. and Industry Canada define frequency usage and assign operating frequencies to individual railroads. Large railroads may be assigned dozens of frequencies due to the high volume of their radio traffic.

These frequency assignments are geographically exclusive and permanent to prevent interference to other rail lines and to avoid expensive and confusing system-wide frequency changeovers. To facilitate interline or "runthrough" operations, locomotives are equipped with multifrequency radios.

Large railroads manage their frequency assignments by permanently allocating frequencies for specific tasks and operations, e.g., road, yard, maintenance, police, etc. Radios are set up to operate on multiple frequencies for interoperational communications and to permit users to switch frequencies when channels become congested.

VHF, UHF, and SHF (microwave) radio waves tend to propagate (travel) in a line-of-sight or straight-line fashion. Therefore, receiving antennas must be able to "see" transmitting antennas for best results. Trees, buildings, hills, etc. can block radio waves, causing poor or noisy transmissions. This is why antennas are typically located on hills, bridges, rooftops, water tanks, towers, and other elevated places. Under normal circumstances, transmission ranges of 100 miles are possible.

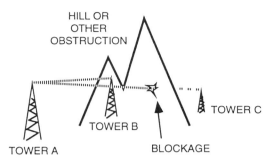

Line-of-sight propagation. Since Radio Tower A can "see" Tower B, signals travel freely between the two. Because Tower C is obstructed by the hill, signals are blocked, resulting in non-existent or poor reception.

In general, transmission ranges can be maximized by raising transmitter power, increasing receiver sensitivity, increasing antenna height, and using directional (gain) antennas. Contrary to popular belief, day-to-day weather conditions such as wind and temperature have no marked effect on VHF transmission ranges, although dense fog and heavy rain or snow can weaken signals, especially at UHF and SHF frequencies.

Seasonal weather characteristics, however, can sometimes increase VHF transmission ranges into the hundreds of miles, particularly in the Gulf Coast, Atlantic Seaboard, Great Lakes, and Mississippi Valley regions. In addition, heavy solar activity, in the form of sunspots or geomagnetic storms, can affect transmission range at any location and time by either boosting it into the thousands of miles or limiting it to a few blocks.

In general, VHF and UHF propagation isn't completely predictable due to the many variables typically found in VHF and UHF systems: transmitter power, antenna types, receiver sensitivity, terrain, physical obstacles, etc. Mobile and portable operation only complicate matters because characteristics change as operating locations change.

There are no hard and fast rules when it comes to VHF and UHF radio systems; every system has its own "personality" that is determined by the above variables. System engineers attempt to overcome possible limitations by designing overly conservative systems with wide performance margins for antennas, transmitters, receivers, and other components.

Unlike VHF and UHF, SHF microwave propagation is very predictable due to careful system design and the stationary nature of microwave installations. Because microwave radiation can be sharply focused, transmitting and receiving antennas (commonly called dishes) must be precisely aligned for optimum transmission characteristics.

To compensate for the blocking effects of rain and fog, microwave transmitter power levels are designed to overcome these obstacles under worse-case conditions. Since microwave systems transmit voice and data exclusively among fixed installations, they're often referred to as "point-to-point" networks.

All railroad radio communications (except CB) are conducted in the FM (frequency modulation) mode. Like FM radiocasts, reception remains relatively quiet when compared to AM and CB radio transmissions (which use amplitude modulation) during thunderstorms and in vehicles with defective, noisy ignition systems.

Unlike FM radio broadcasts, which are transmitted in wideband stereo (50–15,000 Hz audio response) for maximum fidelity, railroad voice communications are conducted in the narrowband, monaural FM mode (300–3,000 Hz response). This allows for more channels per band at the expense of fidelity, which doesn't create problems due to the utilitarian nature of railroad communications.

CHAPTER 2

Modern Railroad Radio Systems

Dispatching Centers

A dispatching center is the heart of a modern railroad radio communication system. On larger roads, multiple train dispatchers monitor rows of video displays to track the locations and movements of trains over the rail system *(see front cover)*. Dispatchers are responsible for the safe, efficient movement of all trains within their assigned operating districts.

To keep trains moving efficiently, dispatchers carefully plan train movements. Fast trains must be allowed to overtake slower trains, and opposing movements must be set up and timed to allow trains to meet and pass one another on adjacent tracks. To accomplish these tasks, dispatchers line remote-controlled track switches and activate lineside signals to control train movements. To ensure smooth operations, they keep in constant touch with train crews and maintenance personnel by radio.

In addition to train dispatchers, dispatching centers usually contain additional dispatching "desks" for police and maintenance activities. Normally, all desks send and receive radio

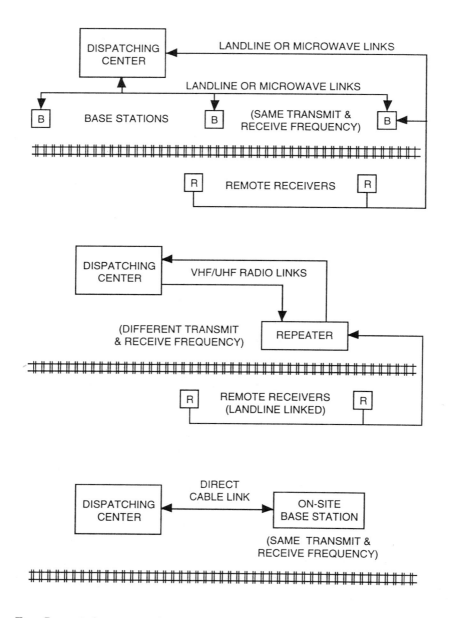

Top: *Base station communication system; all field radios transmit and receive on the same frequency.* Middle: *Repeater-based system; field radios transmit on the repeater input frequency and receive on the repeater output frequency.* Bottom: *Single, on-site base station; used by shortline and industrial railroads; all radios communicate on the same frequency.*

messages via telephone lines or microwave radio links that eventually connect to remote radio receiver-transmitters (base stations) located across the railroad system.

On smaller railroads such as shortlines, remote-link base stations are not used, as these roads require a smaller radio coverage area. Normally, the dispatcher transmits and receives through a repeater (another type of remote receiver–transmitter) or a single, on-site base station.

Base Stations

Base stations form the backbone of large radio communication systems. On larger railroads, hundreds of remote base stations are used. Since base stations are designed to cover wide areas (up to 100 miles), transmitters are usually high powered (up to 350 watts) and use antenna systems that provide coverage in specific areas. In many cases, antennas are set up to provide bidirectional coverage along the railroad right-of-way.

The dispatcher audio transmitted by remote base stations is supplied through telephone lines, point-to-point microwave links, or a combination of both. This is why trackside radio shelters, or bungalows, are often connected to local telephone lines. On smaller railroads with a single base station, the audio is usually supplied on-site directly from a microphone.

On roads with multiple base stations, dispatchers can selectively activate bases to communicate with personnel in specific areas. For instance, to reach a particular train crew, the dispatcher activates the base station closest to the train using a computer keyboard or a touch-sensitive video display at his control console. He then calls the train by its train number or symbol, and if the crew is monitoring the road frequency, which they normally must do, they will receive the message.

Top: *Two-channel base station, two antennas, one per channel; the bungalow houses the base station/repeater unit.* Bottom: *Aerotron model MPAC Base Station/Repeater unit; 12–channel VHF/UHF operation, 10–100 watt output, adjustable; 0.35 µV receive sensitivity (12dB SINAD), 100dB selectivity, 85dB intermodulation; all specs VHF.* (Courtesy Aerotron-Repco Sales)

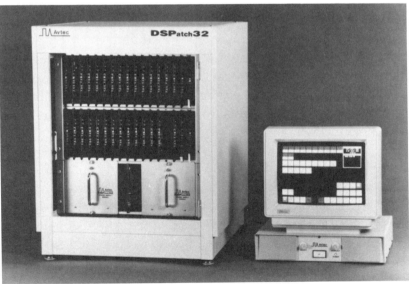

Top: *Andrew model UMX multiband microwave antenna for point-to-point communications.* (Courtesy Andrew Corp). Bottom: *Avtec communication control system. The touch-sensitive video screen (right) is used by dispatchers to activate base stations and telephone circuits.* (Courtesy Avtec, Inc.)

Base stations also double as receivers to route radio communications from train crews, maintenance forces, the police, and other railroad personnel to the dispatcher. These transmissions are normally returned through activated base stations and their associated telephone or microwave links.

Repeaters

A repeater boosts signals by automatically retransmitting any signals it receives. By retransmitting signals at a higher power level or into a specific location such as a tunnel, the repeater increases the range and effectiveness of low power or distant radios. For this reason, repeaters are sometimes called boosters or relays.

Passive repeaters consist of two electrically-connected directional (aimable) antennas. Passive repeaters are used to fill in small "holes" in the coverage area such as inside short tunnels or large cuts. Typically, one antenna is aimed toward the nearest base station, repeater, or remote receiver as necessary, and the other into a tunnel or cut. Normally, trains operating in these areas are not within line-of-sight of a radio facility, so the passive repeater acts as a mirror to reflect radio signals into and out of the hole.

Inside long tunnels, steel-frame buildings, and concrete structures (which all tend to block or absorb radio waves), "leaky" cables are sometimes used to radiate and receive radio waves. These cables are snaked around inside the desired coverage area and connect to an external antenna to ensure reliable communications to and from any point within the structure.

Active repeaters consist of a receiver with its audio output fed into a high power transmitter, the output of which is activated whenever the receiver picks up a signal. An active repeater station is usually located so that its receiver picks up as many signals as possible and its transmitter reaches as many radios as possible.

This means that repeater antennas are typically located at high elevations and are centrally located within the intended coverage area. An antenna covering a rail yard, for example, is often attached to a lighting tower located in the center of the yard.

As with base stations, larger railroads may use hundreds of repeaters across the system, whereas smaller roads may use one or two or none at all—recall that the smallest roads often transmit and receive directly through a single base station. Some railroads also use small, vehicle-based repeaters that boost signals transmitted by nearby low-power radios.

Because active repeaters typically use a single antenna for both transmitting and receiving, the antenna must transmit and receive simultaneously. To do so, the transmit and receive frequencies must be different (resulting in what is called semi-duplex operation) and spaced far enough apart to allow the use of a duplexer, a device that isolates the transmitter output from the receiver input. Without a duplexer, the high power transmitter output would destroy the receiver.

The frequency that the repeater "listens" to is called the input frequency and, not surprisingly, the frequency on which it transmits is called the output. A well-designed repeater in a good location allows even the lowest-power radios to communicate with others located up to 100 miles away. This capability makes active repeater operation popular in large yards and with train crews, maintenance forces, and dispatchers on smaller roads and shortlines.

To work with a repeater, radios must be capable of operating on the repeater's input and output frequencies. On newer ra-

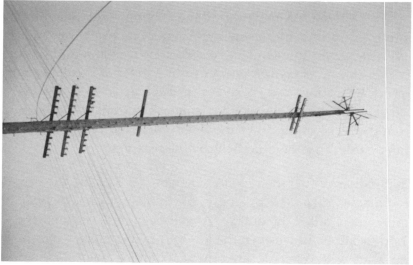

Top: *Base station/repeater antennas including two dipole arrays (on tower) and several collinears (mounted on posts). (Courtesy Sinclair Technologies).*
Bottom: *Base station antenna consisting of a pair of VHF corner reflectors arranged to radiate a bi-directional pattern along a railroad right-of-way. The antenna feedline drop is attached to the pole below the lowest crossarm. The open wire lines, which carry signal, telephone, and power circuits, are not associated with the antenna installation.*

dios, these are selected using standard AAR channel designators *(see Appendix B)*. For example, to operate with a repeater transmitting on 161.535 MHz and receiving on 161.325, users would select "81" and "95" for transmit and receive, respectively, on their radios. This is done using the radio's keypad or rotary selector switches.

With repeater operations, if two or more radios transmit simultaneously on the repeater input frequency, the transmissions interfere with each other and produce a garbled repeater output. Furthermore, when a radio is transmitting, its receiver is disabled and no messages can be received.

Many repeaters cannot be accessed by radios unless a coded squelch signal—known as a continuous tone coded squelch signal (CTCSS) or Tone Private Line™ (TPL™)—is transmitted along with the radio signal. The coded squelch signal is used to unsquelch the repeater's receiver. If the squelch signal is not present, the repeater's receive audio remains muted and therefore, the repeater is not activated.

Coded squelch signals are usually transmitted as a continuous subaudible tone, i.e., at an audio frequency that is low enough that it cannot be heard on ordinary radio equipment *(see Appendix C)*. Some radios use a digital code (such as Digital Private Line™ or DPL™) instead of a tone to access the repeater. A digital code sequence is transmitted at the beginning of the message (producing a "squawking" sound) to unsquelch the system receiver. The squelch is reset at the end of the transmission and cannot be broken until another valid DPL code is received.

The coded squelch system allows railroad personnel to communicate with each other without disturbing the dispatcher. The repeater input frequency is used for local simplex (same receive-transmit frequency) communications, but all coded squelch functions are disabled to mute the repeater input. Only those radios operating near the dispatching center would be heard by the dispatcher.

When using a receiver with a coded squelch, users must be sure the frequency is clear before transmitting. Otherwise, "doubling" will occur, resulting in garbling and interference. To prevent this, coded squelch radios are equipped with a channel "busy" indicator or a monitor button that temporarily disables the coded squelch.

Mobiles

Mobile radios are used in locomotives, cabooses, police cars, and maintenance vehicles and usually transmit enough power to reach base stations and repeaters.

To call dispatchers in a base station system, mobile users must first establish a link to the dispatching center via the nearest base station. If the dispatcher is busy with another call, a link cannot be established. This ensures that only one transmission at a time reaches the dispatcher to avoid confusion and misunderstandings.

To establish a link, the user must ensure his radio is set to transmit and receive on the proper frequency. All base station systems operate in simplex using a single frequency for both transmitting and receiving. With simplex operation, only one transmission at a time can be heard. If two or more radios transmit simultaneously, the transmissions interfere with each other and become garbled. Also, when a radio is transmitting, its receiver is disabled and no messages can be received.

Newer radios indicate or display transmit and receive frequencies using the AAR channel codes. For example, to communicate on a base station system operating on 160.800 MHz, the user would select "46" for both the transmit and receive frequencies on his radio.

The user would then enter an access code for the nearest base station into the radio, and then press the radio's call button. The code usually consists of two numbers or letters and is entered using the radio's keypad or rotary selector switches.

After the call button is pressed, the code is transmitted either as a series of dual-tone, multifrequency (DTMF) tones, or Touch-Tones™, or as a data burst which produces a "squawking" sound. The data burst sometimes includes identification data for automatic unit ID and tracking systems.

If the base station was properly accessed and the dispatcher is not busy with another call, a link is established and an acknowledgement tone is transmitted to the dispatcher and the calling radio. The user can then call the dispatcher and wait for a response. Since dispatchers are usually swamped with work, including solving problems over the telephone, responses are often delayed, much to the annoyance of harried conductors and maintenance personnel.

Once a link has been established, all radios within range of the activated base station can communicate with the dispatcher. At the conclusion of communications, the dispatcher clears the link and waits for another call. While awaiting calls, the dispatcher can monitor any base station of choice, without missing other calls, by making the appropriate selection at his control console.

If users wish to communicate on the base station frequency without disturbing the dispatcher, they would simply transmit without activating any base stations. This permits "off-line" communications without the risk of missing important calls from the dispatcher.

Top: *Aerotron Alpha 1700 locomotive radio; features 25–45 watt transmitter output; 24 VHF channels and 22 dispatcher access codes; 0.35 µV receive sensitivity (12dB SINAD); 90dB receive selectivity; DTMF keypad; data burst transmission capability; CTCSS encoding and decoding.* (Courtesy Aerotron-Repco Sales, Inc). Bottom: *Cab of Electro-Motive model GP-60 locomotive showing control desk and radio handset (left). The radio is recessed into a control panel above the windshield.* (Courtesy AT&SF Railway Co.)

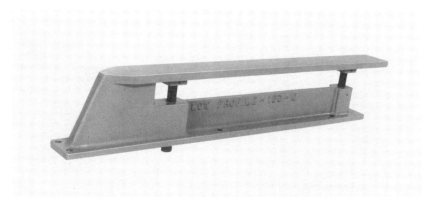

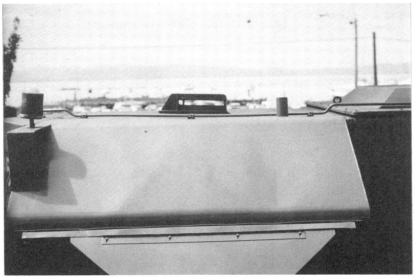

Top: *Antenna Specialists model ASPB579 low profile VHF antenna; cast aluminum construction, 100 watt power handling capacity, tunable; size, 4.1 inches tall, 2.1 inches wide, 21.0 inches long. Mounts with screws and weatherproof gasket.* (Courtesy Antenna Specialists Company).

Bottom: *Low profile antenna mounted on the cab roof of an Electro-Motive model GP-40 locomotive. A smaller (2.5 inches high, 2.5 inches wide, 6.3 inches long) UHF version of the low profile antenna is often used for EOT transmissions.*

Top: *Low profile antenna mounted on cab roof of an Alco model C-424 locomotive.* Bottom: *Low profile antenna mounted on the roof of a General Electric Super 7 locomotive (centered on the boxy protrusion at the rear of the cab). The tower adjacent to the building supports a repeater antenna.*

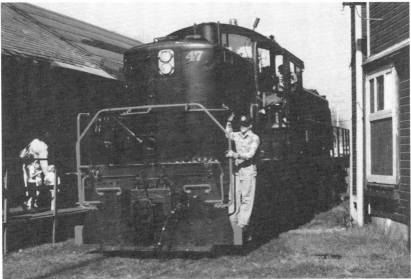

TL: *Low profile antenna centered on cab roof of a General Motors model GP-9 locomotive.* TR: *Antenna Specialists model ASP-16 railroad antenna; 158–163 MHz; 100 watts; brass; 11.4 in. tall.* (Courtesy Antenna Specialists Co). Bottom: *"Firecracker" on cab roof of an Alco model RS-1; note feedline in front of windshield; a whip is also used, between the firecracker and the strobe light.*

Modern Railroad Radio Systems • 35

Vehicular radios. Top: Vertex model FTL-2011 wideband mobile radio; 40 watt power output; up to 24 channels, 134–174 MHz; programmable tone and digital coded squelch capability; optional DTMF keypad on microphone (connector at lower left-hand corner); 0.25 µV receive sensitivity (12dB SINAD); 75dB selectivity; 70dB intermodulation.

Bottom: Vertex model FTL-8011-P3 800 MHz trunked mobile radio; 15 watt power output; ten system, 100 group capacity, 806–866 MHz; programmable tone and digital coded squelch capability; conventional operating mode; 0.30 µV receive sensitivity (12dB SINAD); 75dB selectivity; 70dB intermodulation (see Chapter 7 for information on trunked radio systems and operation).

(Both photos courtesy Yaesu U.S.A.)

On locomotives, antennas are almost always mounted on the cab roof and often take the form of a pipe-like object nicknamed the "firecracker." Other locomotive antennas include whips, low profile models, and radome or "fin" types. Vehicular antennas are usually whips mounted on the vehicle's roof or trunk. Operators normally use handheld microphones in automobiles and, in locomotive cabs, telephone-style handsets to help overcome environmental noise.

Portables

Portable radios, also known as Handie-Talkies™, handhelds, bricks, and lunch buckets, are used by train crews, maintenance forces, and police personnel when operating "on the ground." Typical portable output power is in the range of 5–10 watts, and therefore, coverage area is very limited, normally no more than a mile or two.

In some instances, transmitted signals fall short of a base station or repeater and therefore do not reach the dispatcher. Since most portable communications are intended for other nearby radios, such as when members of a train crew or maintenance gang communicate with each other, this usually does not pose a problem.

However, when portable users need to communicate with dispatchers or other distant stations, the range of a portable radio can often be extended by boosting its signal strength with a local repeater or by inserting it into an amplifier unit. For repeater operation, portables are often pre-loaded with several frequency pairs for "one-knob" selection of multiple repeaters.

In locations with concentrated low-power radio traffic and limited frequency assignments, such as yards, coded squelch techniques are often used to target radio transmissions to particular individuals or departments. Personnel receive only pertinent messages, eliminating the need monitor a never-ending stream of radio traffic.

All handheld portable units feature built-in antennas and microphones, although a remote speaker-microphone unit is often used to facilitate operations in noisy areas. This device is clipped to the user's collar and includes a transmit switch. For hands-free operation, handhelds are often strapped to the user's chest or waist. All handhelds are battery-powered and use interchangeable, rechargeable battery packs.

When cabooses are used on trains—which is becoming increasingly rare—rear-end crewmen operating on the ground use special extended-range "lunch buckets" to communicate with the front end of long trains. Because these units provide up to 15 watts output, they are larger and heavier than handhelds and are normally carried with a shoulder strap.

Lunch buckets usually don't have built-in microphones, necessitating the use of external microphones or telephone handsets. In many instances, longer antennas are used to help increase range. Because of their potentially high transmit current drain, lunch buckets are usually powered by multiple lantern batteries or a surprisingly large number of D cells. During the days of heavy caboose usage, hundreds of these spent batteries could be found discarded along rail lines.

Remote Receivers

Stand alone remote receivers are sometimes used on larger roads to allow lower-powered mobile and portable units—which may otherwise be out of range of a base station or repeater—to communicate with the dispatcher. Even the trans-

Top: *Ready for use: Lunch bucket portable with "rubber duckie' antenna and mobile-style microphone. Some lunch buckets use long, extended-range antennas and telephone-type handsets.*

Bottom: *Locomotive crewmen carrying lunch bucket portables with an over-the-shoulder carry strap.*

Top left: *Vertex model VX-500 VHF portable. Most newer portables, such as this one, can be ordered with an optional DTMF keypad; the blank space below the speaker grille is reserved for this purpose.* (Courtesy Yaesu U.S.A.) Top right: *Repco model RPX450 VHF/UHF portable; 1–6 watt output, 6 channels; 0.30 µV receive sensitivity (12dB SINAD) and 80dB selectivity at 136–174 MHz.* (Courtesy Aerotron-Repco Sales). Bottom: *Internal construction details for "rubber duckie" portable antennas.* (Courtesy Larsen Electronics, Inc.)

missions from higher-powered units can become noisy when they're operated in "blind spots" (locations where radio signals don't radiate well, like inside a tunnel) or when the transmitter is off-frequency.

Signals received by remote receivers are typically sent to base stations and repeaters over telephone or trackside signal lines. Some systems incorporate a "voting" function that automatically chooses the remote receiver with the best reception and sends only that signal to the receiver.

End-of-Train Devices

End-of-train devices (EOTs) perform two tasks formerly handled by crewmen aboard cabooses, which have been eliminated from most trains: (1) monitoring train line (brake) air pressure at the rear end, and (2) notifying the head end when the rear of the train has stopped or started moving.

EOTs are mounted on the last car of a train and contain a low power, battery-operated transmitter that sends telemetry (coded data transmissions) to a special electronic display unit in the locomotive cab. EOTs also contain motion detectors, and sensors to measure the air pressure in the train's brake line. This data is transmitted every ten seconds or so in bursts that produce a chirping sound when monitored on a standard radio.

Some EOTs provide a rear-end braking capability to give the engineer more stopping power in an emergency. Because the brakes on each car are pneumatically controlled from the locomotive via a common brake line, a blockage in the line can prevent the engineer from applying the brakes on all cars.

In the old days, rear-end crewmen would apply the brakes in this situation. However, with the advent of cabooseless oper-

Pulse Electronics model TX-03 TRAINLINK end-of-train device installed on a gondola. Features include an electronic Highly Visible Marker light (HVM) that turns on automatically in darkness and a SMARTPAK battery pack that monitors battery charge status. The TX-03 monitors train line air pressure, motion, and marker light status (on or off) and sends this information (along with battery status) to a monitor in the locomotive cab. Note UHF antenna on top of unit and connection to train line, below. (Courtesy Pulse Electronics, Inc.)

ation, engineers must apply the brakes remotely from the head end. "Two-way" EOTs contain a radio-actuated air valve mechanism that allows the engineer to initiate a rear-end brake application from the locomotive. In the interest of safety, all trains will eventually carry two-way EOTs.

EOTs operate on frequencies that don't interfere with normal voice traffic. To facilitate interline train operations, most EOTs operate on a common frequency, typically 457.9375 MHz, although Norfolk Southern uses 161.115 MHz. Because EOTs also house a blinking light to alert following trains, they are often called flashing rear-end devices (FREDs), markers, or blinkers.

Radio Alarm Detectors

Radio alarm detectors (RADs), sometimes called "talking" detectors or "draggers," have become common in the last few years, and like EOTs, were invented to perform tasks previously handled by railroad personnel. In general, RADs have replaced the watchful eyes of operators and other trackside observers by electronically checking trains for:

- Dragging equipment—a euphemism for derailed or broken wheels, broken axles, or anything else dragging along the roadway, all of which can damage track, lineside structures, and trains and lead to derailments
- Hotboxes—cars with overheated wheel bearings or journal boxes, which can melt, causing fires, broken axles, and derailments
- Oversized loads and cars that can strike bridges, tunnels, and other structures, resulting in damage and derailments

All major roads use RADs, which are typically located every 10–20 miles along main lines, depending on track topography. After a train passes a RAD, it transmits a radio report to the train crew using an electronically synthesized "voice." RADs typically transmit on the road channel. Each railroad tailors its announcements to suit its particular needs, but most give the location of the detector, usually the town or mile post number, the track number in multi-track locations, and the train status such as "no defects" or "no alarm" when no problems are found.

When problems are detected, the RAD sounds an alarm with a continuous warning tone, followed by a defect announcement or a command to stop the train. The detector also reports the location of the defect, e.g., when a hot box is detected, "hot box, track 2, north side, axle 45." The RAD automatically counts the axles from the front of the train to give inspectors an idea of where the problem lies.

In addition to defect information, RADs sometimes announce train speed, direction, ambient temperature, and axle count. The axle count announcement helps crews confirm proper operation of the RAD's counting mechanism. When a RAD fails or is otherwise out of service, a "detector not working" message is usually transmitted.

When defects are detected, or if the detector is not working, trains must be stopped for a complete inspection or repairs, with offending cars "set out" (left on the nearest siding) if repairs can't be made within a reasonable amount of time. Fortunately, false alarms are rare, but all crews and dispatchers are frustrated from time to time by phantom hot boxes and dragging equipment.

On most railroads, crews must acknowledge RAD reports by announcing inspection results, their train symbol, location,

Top: *Bungalow housing RAD equipment, including radio transmitter (note the radome-style antenna on roof).* Bottom: *Train about to traverse a RAD. The "paddles" running perpendicular to the track pivot when hit by dragging equipment, thus triggering the alarm. The hot box detector (in silver enclosure) is situated between steel guard ramps located on the outside of both rails (one detector per axle bearing).*

etc. These announcements are rarely monitored by dispatchers, although the possibility always exists to keep crews "honest."

Some railroads use coded squelch techniques to make sure defective reports reach the dispatcher. These include using different squelch codes for routine and problem announcements in repeater-based systems, and the automatic transmission of access codes for nearby base stations in base systems. Some RADs transmit additional coded squelch signals to mute base station and repeater outputs, thus reducing interference to these important messages.

Links to the Public Telephone Network

Since the late eighties, cellular telephone use by railroads has increased, much in the same way that "cellphone" use has increased within the general community. Cellphones offer all the benefits of regular radio communications with added privacy and greater connection flexibility.

Cellphone-equipped employees can communicate with anyone with access to the public telephone network, including customers, shippers, suppliers, and co-workers. Railroads use the public cellphone network, a cost effective alternative to establishing and maintaining private systems.

Another radio link to the public telephone network is the PBX (private branch exchange), a switchboard system that allows radio users to make telephone calls from anywhere on the railroad system. PBXs give railroad personnel access to the telephone network in areas where cellular service is unavailable. Because maintenance crews often work in remote areas and need to contact suppliers, landowners, etc., they make extensive use of PBX communications.

Most PBX radiotelephone systems operate in a semi-duplex fashion, i.e., one frequency is used for transmitting signals from field radios to the PBX base receiver, and another is used for transmitting the PBX base output to the field. Because of this, conversations must be conducted in a "give and take" fashion; only one party can speak at a time. When one party speaks, the other cannot be heard. Therefore, if both parties unwittingly speak at the same time, both conversations are lost. This situation is similar to conducting a telephone conversation via speakerphone.

To monitor both sides of a conversation, it would be necessary to tune both frequencies since bases typically do not retransmit field radio transmissions, unlike a straight repeater. A scanning receiver would be useful in this instance since it would automatically switch between the two frequencies.

However, since most telephone calls aren't intended for a general audience, there is normally no need to monitor PBX calls. In many instances, the field side of a conversation cannot be heard anyway, due to the relatively low power output of mobile and portable radios. The PBX base transmits a powerful signal that can be received by field radios in most areas in which a railroad operates, much like a repeater.

To facilitate conversation, PBX systems use voice-activated keying, or vox, to activate transmitters. Normally, the operator must press a transmit button to transmit a message. Vox keying automatically activates the transmitter in response to sounds such as voices, busy signals, ringer tones, etc.

To access the PBX network, the caller must have a keypad-equipped portable or mobile radio. A security code is entered using the keypad to gain access to dialtone, at which time the telephone number is dialed, as with a telephone. If the called party is unfamiliar with radio PBX operations, they are usually instructed to speak only when they hear the calling party say "over," and likewise, are told to say "over" when they are through speaking and are ready to listen.

When the conversation is finished, the radio caller either enters a code with the keypad or presses a button on the radio to hang up. The PBX base usually transmits a tone or series of tones to indicate when the PBX has been reset and is ready to accept another call. Most PBX systems are outbound only, i.e., calls can be placed from field, but not received.

Radiotelemetric Links

To help reduce maintenance expenses, many railroads are replacing cables and open wire signal lines with radiotelemetric links. In addition, the increased availability of advanced, cost-effective satellite communication systems has led some railroads to experiment with satellite-based links.

The majority of radiotelemetric links are low-powered (typically less than one watt) and carry digital data for a variety of applications including track control and signalling, grade crossing obstruction detection, automatic car identification, and computer data handling.

Because these links often carry vital information, transmissions must be accurate and reliable. To achieve a high level of performance, advanced transmission methods such as burst, spread-spectrum, and error correction are employed.

In burst transmissions, large amounts of data are transmitted and received within a very short time frame, e.g., in less than a second. Because burst transmissions are short, they don't take much on-air time, and can be quickly and easily re-sent if noise or other interference corrupts the data.

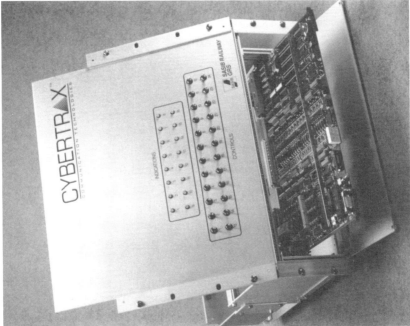

Top: *Safetran R/Link system for replacement of wire-based links in track and signal control systems. Equipment includes (t–b) power supply; track schematic with status indicators; radio transmitter interface; 900 MHz transmitter and (right) input/output module to interface with existing relay-driven systems.* (Courtesy Safetran Systems). Bottom: *Internal view of GRS CYBERTRAX spread-spectrum data radio showing circuit cards; operates from 902–928 MHz.* (Courtesy General Railway Signal Corp.)

To reduce the effects of interference and fading, computer-controlled spread spectrum or frequency hopping techniques are also used to transmit telemetry. These transmissions typically take place in the UHF ranges of 902–928 MHz for freight railroads and 2,400–2,484 MHz (2.4–2.484 GHz) for transit.

During transmissions, the transmitter randomly "hops" or changes frequencies thousands of times a second over a fixed range of frequencies in concert with the receiver. These rapid changes reduce the risk of losing large amounts of data while operating on a single, possibly congested, frequency.

If interference is encountered on one or two hopping frequencies, only a fraction of the data is lost. In this instance, the missing data can often be accurately reconstructed using highly sophisticated error-correction techniques, much as we can mentally fill in missing or garbled words in a noisy telephone call. Some hopping systems "look before they leap" to avoid congested frequencies altogether.

The wireless nature of radiotelemetry opens up many new possibilities for establishing links with moving trains. For instance, some railroads have begun to monitor real-time locomotive performance to anticipate failures and fine-tune maintenance. Otherwise, information would have to be uploaded from on-board computers at maintenance facilities at the time of repair.

Another emerging application for radiotelemetry involves real-time train control and tracking via satellite (GPS) or earth-based transponders embedded below the tracks.

When fed into a multitasking computer system, train location information can be used for a variety of applications such as providing up-to-the-minute car reports for shippers or tracking train locations on high-density lines. By determining the exact locations of trains and feeding this information into computers, fully automatic train dispatching and control is possible, potentially eliminating the need for dispatchers and train crews.

Other applications for positioning technology include studying the effects of track conditions or topography on lading and rolling stock. By electronically mapping the roadway and installing sensors on cars, locomotives, or the loads themselves, the effects of curves, grades, train speed, braking, etc. can be accurately studied and analyzed.

Radiotelemetry plays an important role in the Automatic Equipment Identification (AEI) system currently being implemented in the North American rail network. In the AEI system, lineside sensors read plastic-covered identification tags attached to the sides of all cars, locomotives, trailers, containers, and EOTs in the rail network.

The ID tags electronically store such things as equipment type (locomotive, boxcar, EOT, etc.), road number, and ownership. The information retrieved from the tags is fed into a computer database that tracks car location, mileage, usage, etc. To retrieve information, a trackside sensor beams a UHF radio signal toward each tag as the train rolls by. The radio signal modulates the tags, each of which reflects a modulated signal back to the sensor. Each tag has a unique modulation pattern which corresponds to the data stored for the car or equipment.

Since the power for each tag is supplied by the radio signal itself, the tags do not require batteries. Since radio is used to read the tags, there is no need to keep the tags clean, further reducing maintenance. A previous car ID system, the color bar-based ACI (Automatic Car Identification), failed in the late seventies due to the inability of the system to read dirty color bar tags and the inability of railroads to keep them clean.

Top: *Amtech AEI tag reader in a low profile (sub-railhead) application; sensor unit (right) incorporates the reader antenna; RF module (left) houses the UHF transceiver.* (Courtesy AT&SF Railway Co). Bottom: *OmniTRACS mobile satellite communications system from Qualcomm, Inc. (clockwise from left) radio transceiver unit, satellite antenna (mounted topside of railroad equipment), and Mobile Communications Terminal.* (Courtesy Qualcomm, Inc.)

A new application for the AEI system involves equipment status reporting. By using a tag that interfaces with on-board monitoring equipment, the physical status of car and locomotive components can be monitored and reported. These dynamic tags are called AEM (Automatic Equipment Management) and are read by AEI equipment.

Remote Control Devices

Because of its flexibility, radio is used extensively in remote-control applications including helper locomotive service, industrial switching, and ballast dumping operations.

To help trains over steep grades, railroads often run extra "helper" locomotives in train consists. Ideally, these helpers are placed in middle of the train to distribute tractive forces more evenly along the train. Too many locomotives on the front end can lead to break-in-twos (from exceeding coupling capacity) and "stringlining," a situation in which cars are pulled off the rails when rounding curves. On the other hand, too much shoving power at the rear can compress cars to the point of buckling and derailment.

Although placing units at the middle of a train solves these problems, it creates problems of its own. Adding extra power to the head end poses few problems outside of exceeding coupling capacities because it is a simple matter to connect multiple unit (MU) control cables between the units. However, running MU cables to units located at the middle or end of a train is extremely impractical, if not impossible.

Initially, this limitation posed no problems as railroads were required to run all locomotive consists with a full crew. Crewmen on helper locomotives would control their units in concert with the head end, often by voice command via radio.

However, as railroads began to reduce crew sizes and requirements to cut costs, operations with helper crews became increasingly unattractive.

The existence of the diesel locomotive and reliable radio communications systems made unmanned, remote control operation of helper units feasible in the mid-sixties. In typical operations, the lead locomotive at the head end (the "master") is equipped with the necessary remote control apparatus and receiving/transmitting equipment.

Remote control operation is transparent to the engineer because all control functions are automatically transmitted to the helper units, or "slaves," as the engineer throttles up, applies the brakes, sands the rails, etc. Helpers are equipped with a receiver that monitors the command signals and sends them to the proper locomotive control equipment and a transmitter that sends operational status back to the head end.

Industrial and shortline railroads often use remote control systems to keep crew requirements to a minimum. By wearing a portable control box, a single crewman can control track switches and locomotive functions from anywhere on or around the train, and at the same time couple and uncouple cars, connect brake hoses, release hand brakes, etc. In the same manner, a single operator situated in a control center can operate multiple trains into and out of smelters, storage facilities, humps, and other dangerous locations to eliminate the need for on-site operating personnel.

Roadway maintenance forces sometimes operate ballast hopper discharge chutes via remote control to avoid injuries caused by trips and falls on loose ballast. Without remote control, the discharge is regulated by maintenance personnel walking along the chute as the hopper car is pulled slowly down the tracks. By using remote control, ballast can be released onto the roadbed from a safe distance.

To minimize the risk of accidents, manufacturers of remote control equipment design numerous failsafe security features into their products. To avoid the worst-case scenario in which an operator loses control of a train, resulting in a "runaway," remote systems automatically stop the train when the locomotive moves out of the remote transmitter's range, the control signal becomes corrupted by interference, the control box's tilt ("man down") mechanism is activated, the operator fails to make an operational change for a predetermined length of time, etc.

(Interestingly, some railroads, such as the Vermont Railway, place a life-like dummy in the locomotive cab to minimize "runaway train" calls from uninformed citizens.)

Despite these safeguards, accidents have occurred, prompting some localities and states (like West Virginia) to prohibit or limit remote control operations. To be fair, remote control systems have probably prevented many more accidents than they've created, such as in dangerous environments or when switching long strings of cars in fast-paced yards.

Since an engineer in a locomotive cab often can't see the rear of the train or between cars, he relies on radio communications and hand signals from his brakemen to know what's going on. One miscommunication can send the train off the end of the tracks or into another car, injuring unsuspecting crewmen and damaging goods and equipment. By placing direct control where it's needed most, such as at the end of a backing train, remote control can help to minimize accidents, injuries, and damage.

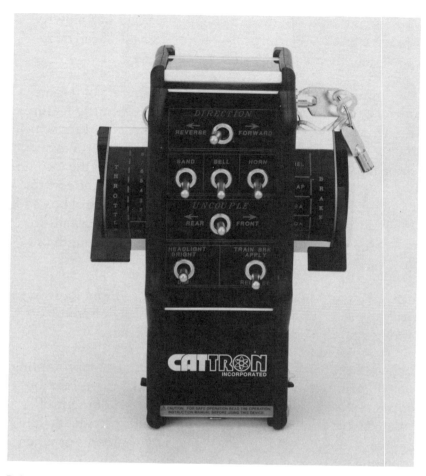

Belt-mounted remote controller. The switches and paddles duplicate the controls found in the locomotive cab. The top panel/switch must be depressed to initiate or maintain locomotive movement. (Courtesy Cattron, Inc.)

The operating range for this type of remote control equipment is typically around a mile. In situations where extra range is needed, such as when controlling long trains, repeaters are used to boost operating range up to three miles. Multiple remote control transmitters for multiple trains can operate on a single frequency using time-division multiplexing (time–sharing) techniques.

CHAPTER 3

Radio Operations

Dispatcher-Train Crew Communications

With the advent of centralized traffic control (CTC), where an entire railroad or major parts of a road are dispatched from single locations, communications between dispatchers and train crews have become the core communication activity. Dispatchers typically communicate with train crews to authorize train movements, ascertain train speed, and to give general instructions and status reports.

Train crews typically communicate with the dispatcher to clarify responsibilities and to report equipment breakdowns, accidents, track conditions, and criminal activity. Crews on different trains also communicate with each other to keep abreast of local track conditions, to relay information on general train conditions, or just to say hello. When trains meet or overtake others, both crews are required to visually inspect the other's train and report any problems. RAD announcements must also be acknowledged upon receipt.

Since crew size reductions have eliminated crew members riding in cabooses and trailing locomotives, intracrew communications are normally conducted only on locals (which use extra crewman, sometimes in a caboose, to drop off, pick up, and switch cars along the line) or when manned helper locomotives are used to shove trains over steep grades.

Local and line-haul train crews normally communicate with dispatchers through base stations and repeaters operating on a main "road" frequency. On larger roads, each operating district may use its own frequency. In many instances, inter and intracrew communications are also conducted on the road frequency to avoid missing calls from the dispatcher.

Yard Operations

Since major yards are busy places, they generate large volumes of radio communications, often on multiple frequencies, each representing a specific yard operation—hump, pulldown, inbound, outbound, etc. Major yards often perform ancillary functions such as car and locomotive maintenance, repair and inspection; radio and communication electronics maintenance and repair—each using its own radio frequency and, quite often, its own repeater.

Because yard and road train operations often overlap (such as when a local or line-haul train enters a yard), it is quite common for mainline crews to communicate with yard personnel on yard frequencies, or for yard crews to contact the dispatcher on the road frequency, and many other combinations.

Yard train crews perform many of the same tasks as local crews (throwing switches, coupling cars and brake hoses, etc.) and therefore generate similar communications. Yard crews usually communicate with a yardmaster (as opposed to a dispatcher) to receive instructions and to get permission to enter and leave certain tracks or areas of the yard.

Yards employ specialized methods of switching or classifying cars to make up a train. Smaller yards "flat switch" cars by "pulling down" cars past a network of switches and then reversing direction to shove or "drill" them into the proper yard tracks. Larger yards use gravity to classify cars by slowly pushing long strings or "cuts" of cars over a small hill called a "hump." Individual cars are uncoupled and allowed to roll down the hump through a network of switches to their proper yard or "bowl" tracks.

The cars are pushed over the hump by a special locomotive set, either manned or remote-controlled. Cars or cuts of cars are uncoupled by a person known as a "pin puller." The cars are then directed to the proper bowl tracks through a series of remote-controlled switches by another person called the "humpmaster," who sits in a control tower along the top of the hump.

To keep cars from speeding through the switches and crashing into cars in the bowl, another person, the "hump conductor," usually located immediately below the humpmaster, uses mechanical retarders that clamp onto either side of the car wheels to regulate car speed. Finally, if a car slows too much and fails to clear the switches or is placed on the wrong track, a free-running flatswitching crew is usually available on short notice to make "pull moves" or "trim moves" to pull cars into the bowl or push cars through the retarders, respectively.

Both moves disrupt hump operations and are therefore performed as quickly as possible. Trim moves are typically ordered by the hump conductor, while pull moves are ordered by a "bowlmaster," the person responsible for the status of cars entering and leaving the bowl.

Top: *Hump locomotives back a cut of cars into the bowl. The locomotives are traversing a set of mechanical speed retarders, which can also be seen on the adjacent tracks.* Bottom: *View from a yard tower showing equipment storage tracks. Note the low-profile antennas mounted on the roofs of the cabooses (on the cupola on the far caboose and above the "N" on the near unit). The locomotives (Montreal Locomotive model C-630) have been stored serviceable, awaiting the next upswing in traffic levels.*

Maintenance Forces

Maintenance-of-way crews inspect, repair, and maintain track, switches, cars, locomotives, buildings, bridges, signals, and communication systems.

Because of the far-flung and broad nature of maintenance activities, maintenance crews communicate with just about everyone on a railroad—dispatchers, yardmasters, roadmasters (in charge of roadway maintenance, or maintenance-of-way), wreckmasters (in charge of cleaning up derailments and other wrecks), trainmasters (in charge of train crews), train crews, and of course, with each other.

As with yard operations, the various maintenance forces often communicate on their own frequencies using their own systems, typically bases, repeaters, and PBXs.

Typical maintenance communications include trouble dispatch calls, maintenance status reports, and calls to vendors and suppliers through a PBX. Track maintainers typically stay in close communication with the dispatcher since they must perform their tasks in the presence of trains—and must obtain permission from the dispatcher to occupy sections of track or to pass stop signals.

Some track maintenance and most wreck-clearing activities are performed by contractors such as Sperry, Pandrol-Jackson (formerly Speno), Loram, and Hulcher. These companies typically use the host railroad's radio frequencies while performing their work. During wrecks and derailments, a huge volume of directives and instructions is transmitted among work crews, wreckmasters, roadmasters, and dispatchers.

Top: Contract maintenance locomotive on a track undercutting (lowering) project. Note the pair of unpainted low profile antennas on the roof (to the left of the horns and on the large boxy structure next to the middle grille). The locomotive is a modified (special cab) version of the Electro-Motive model F40PH passenger diesel. Bottom: Track ballast machine parked on a team track. Note the low profile antenna mounted on the cab roof; it appears much larger due to the relatively small size of the machine.

Police

Most large and medium-sized railroads deploy their own police forces to combat trespassing, theft, and vandalism. In most cases, police communications are relatively sparse. However, as with maintenance activities, communications tend to increase greatly during accidents, derailments, or incidents of major vandalism.

Police communications encompass a wide variety of topics. It is not unusual to hear reports on such things as locomotive, car and lineside fires; chemical spills; runaway cars and locomotives; grade crossing accidents, and other collisions and derailments.

Trespassing incidents are also common and include attempted and successful suicides, personal injuries due to collisions with trains; accidents with dirt bikes and all-terrain vehicles; people walking, sleeping and driving on the tracks, climbing signal bridges and towers, and hopping trains.

No less amazing are reports of vandalism: Theft of all manner of railroad property, such as copper wire and merchandise in boxcars and trailers; stonings and shootings of locomotives, cabooses, and passenger cars; all kinds of objects placed on the tracks or between switch points; thrown track switches; broken or shot-out grade crossing and lineside signals and telegraph insulators; broken crossing gates; break-and-enter of lineside bungalows; and intentional shorting of open wire and track circuits to interfere with signal and train operations.

Typically, the police receive radio reports directly from the police dispatcher's desk or from train dispatchers. They also communicate with each other and with local agencies, but rarely communicate directly with maintenance or train crews.

Taxis

Sometimes called jitneys or limousines, taxis are used to ferry train crews to and from trains that have broken down or are otherwise parked away from crew terminals. In the old days crews would often "outlaw" or exceed the federally mandated 12 hours-of-service law ("hog law") at inconvenient places along the line. To get fresh crews to the trains and retrieve the outlaws, taxis would sometimes travel scores of miles to unfamiliar locations. The hog law has since been changed to require railroads to get crews into terminals before outlawing.

Taxi companies usually sign contracts with railroads to provide their services. The agreement usually includes the use of the main road channel to receive directions and instructions from the dispatcher. In addition to "dogcatching" (retrieving outlawed crews), taxis often shuttle crew members from the rear of long trains to the head end, such as when a crew member must stay behind to re-line a switch or a derailer (installed to keep cars from rolling onto the main) after a train leaves a siding.

Transmitter Identification

Because the FCC and Industry Canada require base station and repeater users to periodically identify themselves, most systems transmit automatic identifications. These transmissions, which usually consist of the station's callsign, e.g. KCE546 or KA3502, given in high speed Morse code, can be decoded and compared to train service license files to identify the frequency, railroad, location of transmitter, and license expiration date.

CHAPTER 4

Scanners and Monitoring

The availability of attractively priced, quality radio equipment has made it possible for even the smallest shortline, industrial, or tourist operation to adopt radio communications. Because of this, the airwaves are filled with all types of railroad communications. By monitoring these transmissions, railfans, radio enthusiasts, and even railroad professionals can gain greater insight into the operational aspects of the railroad industry—much more so than by simply watching trains.

How is it Done?

The simplest and most effective way to monitor railroad radio communications is with a scanning receiver, more commonly known as a scanner. A scanner is a radio receiver that continuously scans or checks a group of user-selected frequencies for the presence radio transmissions.

When a scanner detects a transmission, it stops on the active frequency to allow the user to hear it. When the transmission ends and the channel becomes clear, the scanner resumes its search for another active frequency. To prevent annoying hiss and noise (like an FM radio receiver tuned between stations), all scanners remain muted, or squelched, until a transmission is received.

The main advantage of a scanner is its unique ability to monitor multiple frequencies quickly and efficiently. A listener wishing to continuously monitor multiple frequencies with a conventional receiver would have to constantly adjust the receiver's tuning to all desired frequencies for hours on end, a very tedious, if not impossible, task.

Fortunately, scanners automate this tuning procedure. Today's scanners are available in portable, mobile, and base configurations and can scan up to 2,000 channels at more than 100 channels per second.

What Kinds of Communications Can be Heard?

A scanner lets you listen to most voice-based communications. Non-voice transmissions such as radio remote control, data links, and end-of-train telemetry produce squawks and chirps that are decodable only with the proper receiving or display apparatus. Point-to-point microwave transmissions cannot be monitored due to the specialized nature of microwave equipment and the highly directional characteristics of the transmissions.

Is it Illegal to Monitor Railroad Communications?

Casual monitoring of railroad communications is perfectly legal. Non-casual monitoring, such as listening to the police to facilitate larceny or to be the first on the scene of an accident, is obviously illegal. In some states, it is illegal to use a scanner in a motor vehicle if the scanner is capable of monitoring law enforcement frequencies. There are no such restrictions in Canada.

This law has become somewhat nebulous in recent years due to the popularity of frequency-programmable scanners. Technically, programmable scanners are capable of monitoring law enforcement frequencies, even though none may be programmed in.

Scanner listeners have reported numerous problems with law enforcement officials over the use of scanners in their automobiles. To avoid difficulties, check with local authorities to determine whether or not mobile scanning is permitted in your locale. Otherwise, it's a good idea to keep a low profile when monitoring in any motor vehicle, especially in urban areas, unless you are authorized—as a ham radio operator or public safety official—to use radio communications.

At this time, the only prohibited monitoring activity, per the Electronic Communications Privacy Act of 1986—a largely unenforceable law passed by Congress in response to pressure from the cellular lobby—is listening to cellular telephones and radio pagers. These services are not exclusively assigned to railroads anyway, making them hit-or-miss propositions for hearing rail communications. Canadian listeners are free of such restrictions.

(As an interesting aside, when law enforcement and media personnel intercepted O.J. Simpson's cellular telephone conversations during his infamous and absurd "white bronco" flight, they did so in direct violation of the ECPA).

The only other prohibited activity related to monitoring involves divulging the contents of radio transmissions to others. However, the authorities typically don't pursue the matter unless information is misused, such as to elude police. This is why the popular railroad press routinely prints excerpts and summaries of radio transmissions without retribution.

Railfanning with a Scanner

Over the past dozen years, scanners have become very popular among train enthusiasts or "railfans." Serious railfans use multiple scanners: a base unit at home, a mobile in the car or truck, and a portable for use along the tracks.

Scanners eliminate hit-or-miss railfanning because they provide the information needed to see a maximum number of trains. With a scanner, it's easy to monitor the progress of trains as they roll down the line. Time isn't wasted waiting for trains when none are scheduled or when they are delayed or annulled (cancelled) due to track maintenance, signal failures, derailments, accidents, etc.

Scanners also make it possible to appreciate the people side of railroad operations—everyone keeping trains running in a safe, timely, efficient manner. One needn't be at trackside to enjoy the many facets of railroading; it's possible to be there at any time by simply tuning in.

Advance warning of approaching trains—Perhaps the most popular use of a scanner is to obtain advance warning of approaching trains. By knowing when trains will approach and where they'll be, it's possible to see many more trains, or if desired, only specific trains.

When railfanning in busy areas with many tracks, especially junctions, a scanner can provide information on which tracks will host the next train—and following trains—and when. Even on single tracks with minimal train activity, a scanner is a big help. For instance, if a line runs only a few trains a day, or even a few trains per month, you can show up just in time to see a train and leave immediately afterwards without wasting a lot of time.

Before scanners came into widespread use, the best way to predict the approach of oncoming trains was to get a "lineup" from a lineside operator. If an operator was unavailable, there was no reliable way, other than the marginally effective methods of watching lineside signals and listening for locomotive horns, to monitor train progress. The use of signals is limited to what can be seen, while horns are good only as far as they can be heard. There was usually no way to tell what was going on up the line or on other railroads in the area.

Scanners vastly improve the predictability of approaching trains. By monitoring radio alarm detectors, dispatcher and crew communications, and EOT telemetry, you can get a good idea of train activity in the immediate area as well as across the region.

The most popular advance warning device is the radio alarm detector. Because RADs are activated by passing trains, they are an excellent source of information. If multiple RADs can be monitored, information can be obtained on trains approaching from multiple directions and at great distances, depending upon reception range.

In some cases, receiving too many detectors on a busy day can become confusing because trains activate detectors as they come and go, perhaps on multiple tracks. For example, it's easy to mistake a westbound train passing a RAD to the west as an approaching eastbound. To avoid this confusion, listen carefully to RAD announcements and crew acknowledgements. RADs usually announce track numbers and locations, and crews often respond with their train number or symbol and the number of the lead locomotive.

Even in areas without RADs or RAD reception, it's possible to gather large amounts of intelligence by monitoring dispatchers, train crews, maintenance personnel, etc. On many roads, if a train radio can be heard, chances are a train is nearby, perhaps up to ten miles away. On many roads, train crews are required to "call out" signal aspects and locations over the air.

If train radios can't be heard, it's still possible to get a good idea of the train situation because dispatchers periodically transmit train orders; check train locations; authorize trains to occupy sections of track (which are sometimes given place names); transmit status reports to maintenance crews; etc. However, be forewarned: Some trains do not communicate regularly with the dispatcher, and therefore, there's no easy way to predict their approach.

Finally, the telemetric signal emitted by EOTs can be used to signal the approach of a train. On a scanner, the signal produces a periodic "chirping" or "beeping" sound. Because the signal is only intended to travel the length of a train, it is relatively weak. Therefore, if telemetry is heard, a train is often very close. In some instances, the EOT offers little or no warning at all.

Determining what kind of train is approaching—It's often quite easy to tell what kind of train is approaching, but it takes careful listening and some knowledge of train symbols and operations. On larger roads, train symbols are used by train crews and dispatchers to identify trains. Since symboled trains consistently carry the same kinds of loads on a fixed schedule between fixed locations, it's possible to become familiar with the train, including type of freight equipment used and merchandise hauled, over a period of time.

Train symbols consist of letters, numbers, or a combination of both. Letter-based symbols are usually descriptive, representing train type, lading, origination, and destination. For instance, on the Union Pacific, train symbol CBNP-10 means

"Council Bluffs, Ia.–North Platte, Nebr., originating on the 10th of the month." Since CBNP is a general merchandise train, you'd expect to see plenty of boxcars but few piggyback trailers.

Symbols are often prefixed or suffixed with letters and numbers, as the "10" above. In the previous example, this number refers to the date the train was first called. However, for local trains, the suffix usually refers to the train number. Other suffixes in use on the UP include "Z" (piggyback train); "B" (second section of a train when an overflow of freight exists); and "D" (stacktrain). Prefixes include "C" (coal); "L" (local); and "G" (grain).

Most railroads generally follow the same symbolling scheme, for example EDSP, East Deerfield-Springfield, Mass. (Guilford) and OALBT, Oakland–Long Beach trailers (Southern Pacific). For more train symbols and their meanings, see Appendix E for a listing of trains in which car CR889280, a Conrail grain hopper, travelled the Conrail system between March and June of 1994.

Understanding overall operations—When not using their scanners to find out about approaching trains, most railfans monitor all aspects of railroad operations. This can be done trackside, on the road, or at home.

By listening to a wide variety of communications, you can gain a good understanding of all facets of railroading. Fortunately, most communications are routine, but things really turn around when train density exceeds track capacity, equipment breaks down, accidents occur, and when police are called to investigate trespass, theft, or vandalism.

Because scanners are ideal for multi-frequency monitoring, it's not unusual to hear a train crew call in a case of vandalism, such as obstructions placed on the tracks, and then hear the dispatcher contact the police and the appropriate maintenance activity to clear the tracks. If the incident occurred nearby, low-powered portables would be in range, making it possible to hear all subsequent unit-to-unit police and maintenance communications.

Many railfans are ham radio operators and often get together on the air to discuss the latest rail happenings, especially at large rail-related events. Try tuning the following frequencies to hear this activity: 146.490, 146.565, 223.620, 446.050, and 1294.425 MHz.

Buying a Scanner

When buying a scanner for the first time, it's a good idea to start out with a simple setup and then upgrade later on, if you so decide. Otherwise, you may end up paying for features that are of little use to you. When you become familiar with scanners and scanning, you'll have the knowledge and experience needed to expand your setup in a way that suits your needs.

As with most things, when you buy a scanner, you get what you pay for. Generally, the selling price of a scanner is based on channel capacity—the more channels, the higher the price. For example, a new scanner capable of scanning ten channels (a basic unit) can go for as low as $85.00, whereas a full-featured model scanning 2,000 channels can go for more than $500 (used scanners are covered in Chapter 6).

For typical railroad communications, a ten-channel scanner is more than adequate. One or two channels each can be dedicated to road, yard, maintenance, and police activities and still leave room for weather channels, local police and fire departments, etc.

A good configuration for beginners consists of a ten-channel portable, attached antenna, and a plug-in transformer for recharging the batteries and powering the scanner. This setup is usually quite adequate for general purpose listening, such as monitoring road channels if you live within 15 miles or so of an active rail line or if you spend a lot of time trackside.

When shopping for a scanner, you can visit local shops or browse mail order catalogues. Many people won't buy locally because they feel locals tend to charge more for their wares than catalogue stores. While this may be true, especially in smaller towns, remember that the personal service you receive from a local dealer is an important part of the price.

You can ask questions while testing out scanners and accessories in the store and continue to receive in-town support after the sale. Also, local dealers are usually very familiar with the local scanning scene and can offer valuable advice in this area. To find a local dealer, check in the yellow pages under Electronics Equipment, Radio Communications Equipment, Antennas, Television, etc.

Mail order houses sell large volumes of merchandise and as a result, many offer unbeatable prices. Some houses feature toll-free telephone lines for placing orders, but not for product information or support. This can become an expensive proposition should something go wrong with your scanner or relationship with the dealer.

Fortunately, in the interest of providing quality customer service, many mail order houses offer toll-free support lines, attractive warranties, and no-risk (outside of shipping charges) guarantees. These suppliers regularly advertise in radio hobby magazines and occasionally in the popular railroad press *(see Appendix G)*.

Scanner Configurations

Scanners are available in three basic scanner configurations—portable, base, and mobile. Each has its own strengths and weaknesses.

Portables, which are also known as handhelds, are by far the most popular type of scanner in use today. Because of their portability (they are battery-powered and easily carried in one hand), they are very versatile and can be used practically anywhere. Nevertheless, portables do have a few disadvantages.

One of the biggest disadvantages is poor audio quality. To conserve battery power, portables use low-power audio amplifiers, which results in poor sound projection. This is complicated by the necessity of using small loudspeakers which further degrades sound quality. Because portables use small antennas, their signal-pulling capability is limited, adversely affecting reception range.

Finally, the portable's blessing—its battery power—is also a curse because batteries must be periodically inspected and replaced or recharged, depending on the kind of batteries being used. Alkalines are expensive, but have the advantage of being easily field-replaceable—they're usually standard penlight cells. Rechargeable batteries are very cost effective, but must be periodically recharged and can't be purchased at the corner drugstore due to their non-standard designs.

Base scanners are also very popular, but not as much as portables. This is due to the base's biggest weakness: It's simply not portable, but as the name implies, it's not designed to be. All bases are powered by ac line current, and therefore are almost always used indoors.

Left: *Radio Shack PRO-26 portable scanner; 25–1,300 MHz; 200 channels; scans 50 channels/second, AM and wide/narrowband FM; switchable overload attenuator.* Right: *Radio Shack PRO-50 portable scanner; 30–512 MHz; 20 channels.* (Both photos courtesy Tandy Corp.)

Top: *Radio Shack PRO-2042 base scanner; 25–1,300 MHz; 1000 channels; scans 50 channels/second, AM and wide/narrowband FM; switchable overload attenuator.* Bottom: *Radio Shack PRO-2026 mobile scanner; 29–956 MHz; 100 channels, AM/FM; 12Vdc operation.* (Both photos courtesy Tandy Corp.)

Bases have a few major advantages over portables. Obviously, they don't suffer from the handheld's battery problem. In addition, they usually have improved audio quality and projection since power consumption and speaker size are not limiting factors. Finally, base antennas tend to be longer and more effective than portable antennas, and therefore, reception is improved.

Mobile scanners have gained in popularity in the last couple of years, but still lag far behind portables and bases. Still, more and more mobile units are being installed in cars, boats, and RVs. Like bases, the mobile's biggest disadvantage lies in its lack of portability. Another disadvantage is not related to technology, but to the laws limiting mobile scanner use.

Unlike portables, mobiles usually have good audio quality and are powered by motor vehicle electrical systems. They also use external antennas, which improves reception significantly.

Performance Considerations

Manufacturers publish performance specifications or "specs" that describe scanner performance relative to accepted industry standards. Specs are important because they give a rough indication of how a scanner will perform in the real world. In addition to channel capacity, specs describe such things as band coverage, scanning speed, battery drain, audio output, and three important performance considerations: sensitivity, selectivity, and dynamic range. As with channel capacity, expensive scanners tend to offer better performance in these and all other areas.

Sensitivity—Sensitivity is a scanner's ability to receive signals, which becomes important when monitoring in fringe areas, i.e., places where reception is barely possible. In these locations, scanners with better sensitivity will receive weak signals, perhaps noisily, whereas less sensitive scanners won't pick up a thing. Receive sensitivity is usually specified in terms of 12 decibel (dB) SINAD (the ratio of audio signal + noise + distortion to noise + distortion = 12dB) or 20dB quieting (the ratio of radio signal + noise to noise = 20dB).

Sensitivity is rated in the following table.

method	poor	fair	good
12dB SINAD	0.6–0.8 µV	0.4–0.6 µV	0.3–0.4 µV
20dB quieting	0.8–1.0 µV	0.6–0.8 µV	0.5–0.6 µV

These ratings are for VHF high-band frequencies only. Specs vary by band. For example, a 0.7 µV 12dB SINAD spec for UHF reception would indicate good performance. When comparing specs, make sure you look at the VHF high band (around 160 MHz), because this is where most rail systems operate.

Sensitivity is measured in microvolts (µV), or millionths of volts, because the voltage of a radio signal is extremely low. From the table, good sensitivity is considered to be around one-third of a microvolt (0.3 µV). Although this is a minuscule voltage, a scanner with good sensitivity must adequately respond to signals at this level.

12dB SINAD and 20dB quieting tests are used to measure sensitivity. As you know from listening to broadcast stations, weak signals tend to be noisy, whereas strong signals are quiet. A "quietness" level of 12dB SINAD or 20dB quieting is fairly noise-free. Since we have these standards of quietness, it's possible to measure how strong a received signal must be in a particular scanner to reach the standard state of quietness.

If two scanners (A and B) were tested and scanner A needed a 0.8 µV signal to reach a quietness level of 12dB SINAD, but scanner B needed only 0.3 µV, scanner B would be much more sensitive. Scanner B only took a 0.3 µV signal level to reach the standard state of quietness, whereas scanner A took a much stronger 0.8 µV signal. In sum, scanner B is capable of receiving much weaker signals than scanner A, and thus will pick up many more signals.

Selectivity—Selectivity is a scanner's ability to reject signals on nearby frequencies. If a scanner has poor selectivity, you'll hear radio signals from other channels even though you don't have them tuned in.

For example, the Rochester & Southern's repeater transmits on 160.770 MHz, while Conrail's base station transmits on 160.800 MHz—only 0.030 MHz or 30 kHz away. Both signals are strong and clear in the Rochester, N.Y. area. When tuned to Conrail, a scanner with good selectivity would completely reject the R&S signal and it wouldn't be heard. A scanner with poor selectivity would allow the R&S signal to "leak in" to varying degrees, and in worst cases, the R&S signal would be just as strong as Conrail's.

Selectivity is usually measured in terms of how well the scanner rejects a signal located 30 kHz away from the frequency being monitored. This is accomplished by comparing the strength of the two signals—the weaker the interfering signal, the better. This difference is measured in decibels, where higher dB levels mean increased rejection, decreased interference, and therefore, better selectivity.

When comparing selectivity specs, higher dB levels are better than lower ones. However, when making comparisons, make sure the levels are referenced to the same 30 kHz standard. If for some reason the specified frequency spacing is greater, such as 50 kHz, then selectivity specs would look better since the interfering signal is farther away and would be less likely to interfere.

Many scanners have a 50dB selectivity rating at 30 kHz, which means that a signal 30 kHz away is 100,000 times weaker than the desired signal, and therefore probably wouldn't interfere. In the R&S-Conrail example, which represents a 30 kHz channel spacing, Conrail wouldn't be heard while monitoring the R&S, and vice-versa. However, as dB ratings fall, selectivity ratings deteriorate which results in the two signals interfering with each other with increasing strength and clarity.

Dynamic Range—Dynamic range is a scanner's ability to respond to both strong and weak signals. Scanners with good dynamic range react well to a wide range of signal levels and offer good sensitivity without overloading when receiving strong signals. Poor dynamic range can result in overloading, which in turn leads to intermodulation.

Intermodulation is annoying because it produces false signals within the scanner that appear on the frequency being monitored. Sometimes these interfering signals are just as strong and clear as the desired signal. Unfortunately, when tuned to railroad frequencies, powerful paging transmissions tend to overload scanners resulting in a never-ending cacophony of paging tones and voices.

Like selectivity, dynamic range is measured in dBs, with higher levels of dynamic range translating into increased "headroom," and therefore, less intermodulation and interference. Many specifications don't include dynamic range or intermodulation specs, however more expensive scanners tend to subdue intermodulated signals more effectively, approaching 50dB of suppression.

Operating a Scanner

For the beginner, just learning how to operate and program a scanner can be challenging. As with most things, you'll soon become an expert and may wish to explore new ways to maximize the usefulness and effectiveness of your scanner. However, you should have a thorough understanding of the basics before you attempt the advanced techniques described in the next chapter.

Despite everything you've heard about reading instruction manuals, it's absolutely imperative that you read and understand yours to get the most out of your scanner. Unlike VCR instructions, most scanner manuals are easy to understand.

Frequencies—A scanner is useful only if it's set to receive on the proper frequencies. There are three main ways to obtain frequencies.

The easiest and most popular way to find frequencies is to consult a frequency guide *(see Appendix G for information sources; a partial listing of railroad frequencies is given in Appendix A)*. These guides list hundreds of frequencies covering all aspects of railroad operations. Normally, they list all frequencies assigned to a railroad, so some experimenting may be necessary to determine which ones are used in your area. In addition, they usually list the purpose of the frequency (police, road, yard, etc.), but this may require verification as well.

Another good source of information is the local railfan community. This source is especially beneficial because frequencies have already been verified. Most railfans are more than happy to share frequencies, just ask anyone at trackside with a scanner.

Friendly train crews sometimes give out frequencies. Most of today's railroad radios feature a digital readout that displays both transmit and receive frequencies using the standard two-digit AAR channel codes *(see Appendix B)*.

Older radios and some newer handhelds list the transmit and receive frequencies on a sticker attached to the back of the radio. If you manage to get one frequency, you can sometimes locate others because railroad personnel will often verify channel numbers before changing frequencies.

If you do approach train crews, remember they're not obligated to disclose this information, and if they do, they're doing you a favor.

Frequency counters can be used to determine the frequency of any railroad radio transmitter, including portables, bases, and repeaters. Battery-operated, handheld frequency counters have been developed especially for this purpose. When used in close proximity to a transmitter, they display the transmitted frequency on a digital readout.

Because the air is filled with thousands of radio signals, you must be relatively close to the transmitter you are analyzing to get a reading. The distance is proportional to the power of the transmitted signal: The weaker the transmitter, the closer you must be. For a typical portable, 100 feet is usually sufficient.

Most counters only need a few seconds of transmit time to get a reliable reading. Once a reading is made, it can be locked in to avoid losing a reading during short transmissions.

Modern scanners allow you to program or place frequencies into any channel location. For scanners with relatively few channels, i.e., 10–20, it doesn't really matter where frequencies

Optoelectronics Scout frequency counter; records and saves up to 400 unique frequencies from 10–1,400 MHz; records frequencies automatically. A computer-aided scanning interface is available. (Courtesy Optoelectronics, Inc.)

are programmed. Scan times are fast enough to cycle through all channels within seconds. When a transmission ends on a certain channel, the scanner will cycle through in time to receive the response or next transmission on the same channel, unless of course another channel becomes active in between.

To prevent the scanner from stopping on undesired channels between transmissions, channels can usually be "locked out" or skipped during the scan cycle. To guarantee that all responses are heard, the channel of interest can be permanently selected using the manual mode, which deactivates the scan function. On some scanners, it can also be assigned "priority," i.e., whenever the channel becomes active during the scan cycle, it is immediately tuned in.

To help avoid the need to lock out channels and deactivate scan functions, most scanners feature a delay function that prevents the scanner from scanning for a few seconds after a transmission. If the next transmission occurs during the delay, the scanner receives the entire message.

When listening to PBX transmissions, it is sometimes desirable to lock out all channels except the PBX input and output frequencies. Most PBX base stations do not retransmit input signals, therefore both frequencies must be monitored to hear both sides of a conversation. To ensure that both sides are heard, the scan time between the two channels must be minimized. Remember that most input signals originate from low-power radios with limited range, and therefore may not be received.

When using a scanner with scores of channels, frequency management becomes more important because scan cycle times are much longer. Fortunately, "megachannel" scanners are set up in banks of ten or 20 channels each. For instance, channels 1–10 are in bank one, 11–20 in bank two, 21–30 in bank three and so on. Entire banks can be enabled/disabled to optimize scan cycles. Like the ten-channel scanner, individual channels within each bank can be locked out or delayed.

By using channel banks, you can group rail channels according to railroad, function, or any desired combination. For example, bank 1 could be programmed with only road channels for one or several railroads, bank 2 maintenance, bank 3 police, etc. Alternatively, you could scan by railroad by programming single banks with all functions from one railroad.

By disabling banks, you can focus on a particular railroad or railroad function.

Furthermore, if you have a scanner with hundreds of channels, you could program remaining banks with police, fire, cordless phones, marine, or even other railroads that you occasionally visit.

Power Sources—All portable scanners are designed to operate off either disposable or rechargeable batteries. In the long run, rechargeables are more economical than disposables, but must be periodically recharged. Because these batteries are usually housed in non-standard packs that attach directly to the scanner, they can't be purchased from the local drug store if you forget to charge them. Some scanners accept standard-sized rechargeable batteries, including the new rechargeable alkaline cells.

Disposable batteries are convenient to use because they don't require charging and can be purchased just about anywhere. However, if you don't use your scanner for six months or more, you should remove the batteries to prevent leakage and damage, which is often irreparable. Ordinary carbon-zinc batteries are very prone to leakage and should not be used, despite their attractive price. Alkalines are more expensive but last longer and are less likely to leak. If you must use carbon-zincs, inspect them regularly.

Cold weather weakens batteries considerably, especially rechargeables. To keep batteries warm, carry spares in an inside pocket, like under your jacket, but take care not to short the battery terminals with coins, keys, or other metal objects. This creates an explosion or fire hazard. Keep in mind some high speed "drop-in" chargers regulate charging rates according to battery temperature. When charged in cold weather, batteries could overcharge, creating an explosion or fire hazard.

For the ultimate in portable battery performance, self–contained, rechargeable power packs are available to deliver maximum power for long periods of time—more than enough to power a scanner for scores of hours. Like automobile batteries, these employ lead-acid cells (leakproof), although some units are small enough to keep under a jacket to ensure full power in even the coldest weather.

If your portable or base station scanner is capable of operating on 12 volts dc, you can run it or charge its batteries from your vehicle's electrical system. If you're not sure about your scanner's operating voltage, consult the instruction manual. If you don't have the manual, look on the scanner, especially around the power input jack; it may be embossed on the case.

If this fails and your scanner uses regular 1.5 volt batteries, multiply the number of batteries in the scanner by 1.5 to get the operating voltage. If you do have a 12-volt scanner (eight batteries), you'll need a way to tap into the vehicle's electrical system. One of the easiest ways to do this is with a cigarette lighter plug. Normally, you can buy such a plug and cable from the scanner manufacturer. If this is impossible or your lighter doesn't work, you can build your own cable assembly *(see Chapter 6)*.

Most portable and mobile scanners can be powered off standard ac line current. Many scanner manufacturers supply a transformer and cable to do this. If your portable is equipped with rechargeable batteries, you're probably already powering your unit off the ac mains.

If you can't get a transformer assembly from the manufacturer, you might be able to buy one. As discussed previously, you'll need to determine your scanner's operating voltage and in addition, the current draw. Voltage and current are usually specified in the instruction manual or may be printed on the scanner case. If you get the incorrect transformer, both the transformer and your scanner could be damaged.

Current draw and transformer capacity are usually given in milliamps (mA). Make sure you buy a transformer that's capable of delivering the current and voltage necessary to power your scanner. For example, if your scanner draws 25 mA at 12 volts, you'll need to buy a 12 volt dc transformer with a current rating of at least 25 mA. You'll also have to buy a transformer with a plug or adapter that fits your scanner's dc input jack and provides the proper polarity. This is very important—reversing the polarity (i.e., negative for positive) could irreparably damage your scanner.

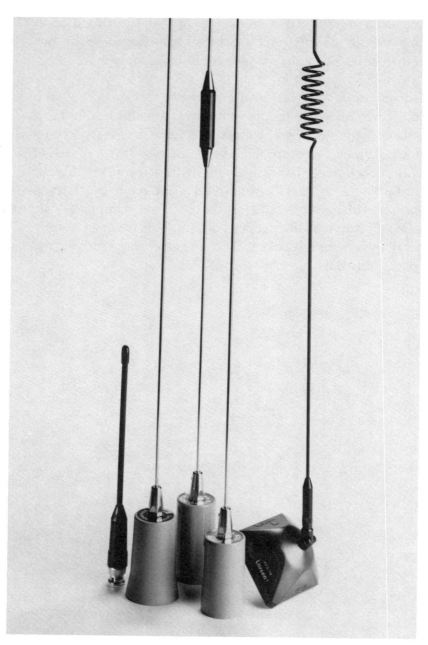

Courtesy Larsen Electronics, Inc.

CHAPTER 5

Improving Scanner Performance

Scanner performance can be improved in several ways. By improving reception, you can increase the clarity and number of transmissions you receive: In addition to receiving an increased number of distant, high-powered transmitters, you'll be able to hear more low-powered, local radios such as portable and mobile units. Furthermore, the flexibility and utility of any scanner can be greatly increased with a variety of add-on accessories.

Reception is maximized by capturing as many signals as possible and feeding them to the scanner with minimum signal loss. This usually means using high quality antennas, feedline, signal amplifiers, or professional-level equipment. The use of professional equipment yields dependable performance under all operating conditions, in addition to providing excellent reception qualities.

When interconnecting antennas, accessories, scanners, radios, etc., the cables and connectors supplied with these units must be compatible. If not, interconnections can be made with a variety of adapters or jumper cables that convert from one style of connector to another.

Antennas

Often seen as an unimportant part of a scanner setup, antennas are extremely important—the greatest scanner in world is absolutely worthless without an antenna. To maximize your scanner's performance, you must use the best antenna possible. Even a poor antenna is better than no antenna.

In some cases, using the antenna supplied with a scanner is just about as good as having no antenna at all, especially when you're monitoring inside a steel or concrete building, inside a car, or in poor reception areas such as valleys, dense forests, or isolated areas.

One of the easiest and most inexpensive ways to improve reception is to replace the fixed-length antenna that comes with your portable or base scanner with a longer antenna, an adjustable whip (also referred to as a telescoping or collapsible whip) or, for base scanning, an indoor wall-mounted antenna.

Portables typically come with a short, flexible, directly attached antenna curiously called a "rubber duckie." *(see page 40)*. While convenient, rubber duckies are not the best choice for pulling in weak signals. They are short, not optimized for railroad frequencies, and cannot be placed for maximum reception without moving the scanner. Base scanners usually come with whip antennas that have similar limitations.

To overcome the problems of rubber duckies and fixed whips, you'll have to accept some degree of inconvenience, i.e., longer antennas, sometimes placed away from the scanner. However, the tradeoff could be well worth your while because longer antennas can bring about a remarkable improvement in reception, especially if they can be located in areas offering maximum reception, such as high along a window.

Any antenna without a loading coil (the in-line, cocoon-like object on the hole mount antenna, page 96; these are also located at the base of the antenna) can be adjusted to optimize reception on a particular frequency or band of frequencies.

Loading coils make it difficult to adjust antennas because there is no way of knowing how much wire is coiled up inside. They shorten the physical length of an antenna to gain a compromise between straight antennas (maximum length), and rubber duckies (minimum length), which are actually loosely spiraled loading coils.

To tune an adjustable whip, slide out telescoping portions until you reach the length indicated by the following formula:

length (inches) = 2800 ÷ frequency in MHz

For example, you would like to maximize reception of Conrail's main road frequency, which is 160.8 MHz. By using the formula, you can calculate optimum antenna length for 160.8 MHz, thus:

length (inches) = 2800 ÷ 160.8,

length (inches) = 17.4

Therefore, to maximize reception on 160.8 MHz, you'd need to adjust your antenna to approximately 17–3/8 inches (don't worry about getting the exact length; you can be off by a half-inch or so without adverse effects). This gives you the length of what is known as a "quarter-wave" antenna.

If you have an antenna that is not adjustable (like many wall-mount and base whip antennas), you can get the same results by trimming or shortening the antenna with wire cutters. The adage "measure twice, cut once" certainly applies here: If you cut the antenna too short, it will be optimized for a frequency higher than your frequency of interest. After cutting fixed whips, be sure to file off any sharp burrs and to place a thimble or styrofoam ball over the end of the antenna.

If you're concerned about errors, you may want to buy another antenna for experimental purposes. This would allow you to practice without destroying the only antenna supplied with your scanner. You may also wish to have multiple antennas maximized for different frequencies. Another alternative would be to buy an adjustable whip for your base, which could be adjusted without cuts of any sort.

Cutting antennas to length will not totally degrade reception on other frequencies. Antennas tuned to railroad frequencies will continue to receive other services, such as police and fire, with little or no loss in signal strength. If you're concerned, you can optimize several antennas for each service.

When using a whip or rubber duckie on a portable scanner, it's sometimes helpful to set the scanner on a metal object such as an automobile hood, pipeline standpipe, guard rail, etc. By doing so, you create a ground plane with which the antenna can work. The larger the surface area, the better. Grounded objects, such as standpipes, tend to work better than non-grounded objects.

All antennas function better with a ground plane because it creates a complete antenna. The rubber duckie on a scanner or the vertical element on an outdoor antenna forms only one half of the antenna—the "hot" element. The other half is formed by a ground, either an earth ground or an artificial ground created by metallic objects. This can be the roof of a car or, for outdoor antennas, three or four horizontal radials evenly spaced in the same plane below the vertical element.

Without an effective ground, antennas simply do not work well; a ground plane can improve reception dramatically.

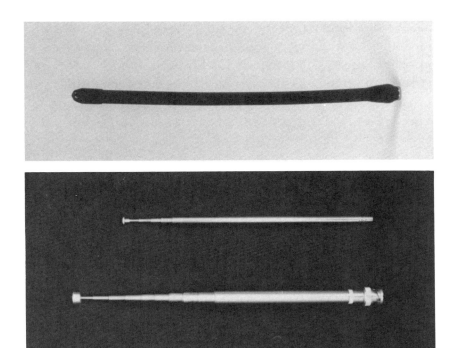

Top: *Austin Condor high performance "rubber duckie" antenna; 12 in. long; improves reception over standard "duckies."* (Courtesy Grove Enterprises, Inc.)
Bottom: *Collapsible whips for base scanners (top) and handhelds.*

When using an adjustable whip, make sure the antenna is kept clear of metal objects. Rubber duckies are insulated with a vinyl or plastic covering, but whips are usually uninsulated. Therefore, if the antenna touches bare metal, like the rain gutter of a car, signals will be lost or attenuated, resulting in degraded reception.

Adjustable whips can make your handheld scanner top heavy, therefore it may tip over unless you hold onto it or prop it up. Stands are available for this purpose. If you prop the scanner by the antenna, remember to insulate it with a rag, piece of wood, or other insulating material if it contacts bare metal.

When using long whips, be careful to keep them away from trackside power and signal lines. These lines are sometimes quite low due to post-construction fill projects and may carry currents of up to 800 volts. Contact with one of these lines will "fry" your scanner and quite possibly kill you. Remember—you can be KILLED if your antenna touches a power line!

The increased popularity of mobile scanning has increased interest in mobile antennas. Mobile antennas behave like whips and can be tuned in the same manner. They tend to work better than portable and base antennas because they take full advantage of the ground plane created by metal automobile roofs and trunks (vinyl roof covering does not affect the ground plane).

There are several types of mobile antennas available, including window mount, trunk lip mount, gutter mount, hole mount, glass mount, magnetic mount, coupled, and even marine antennas. Each has advantages and disadvantages as described in the following paragraphs.

Window mount antennas are temporarily held in place by rolling up the window onto an integral mounting bracket. Some are designed to use rubber duckie antennas, typically removed from the scanner in use. The use of other add-on antennas, such as adjustable whips, is not recommended when the vehicle is in motion, as these aren't designed to withstand high wind speeds. Furthermore, the increased torque created by longer antennas could damage the mount.

Trunk lip mount antennas can be permanently mounted without drilling any holes—they clamp onto the trunk "lip" in the seam directly behind the rear window. This makes cable routing convenient because the feedline enters the vehicle on the inside of the trunk.

Because of their mounting requirements, trunk lip mount antennas won't work on hatchbacks or trucks. In addition, they can't be removed easily which could create problems at the car wash or in high-crime areas. Since mounting is restricted to the trunk area, rooftop mounting—which can improve reception—is impossible.

Gutter mount antennas attach to a vehicle's rain gutter, which is the ridge that runs along the roof on each side of the car above the doors. These antennas can be mounted at the roof for best reception and do not require mounting holes.

One drawback of the gutter mount is that the feedline must be run on the outside of the car and through a window or door to the inside. This sometimes causes problems when windows can't be closed all the way or the feedline gets pinched or crushed in a door or window.

Hole mount antennas can be permanently mounted anywhere on a vehicle, but require mounting holes that can reduce automobile resale and trade-in value. Hole mount antennas have the same permanent mounting disadvantages as trunk lip mount antennas.

Glass mount antennas have become popular because of the cellular telephone boom and are normally glued to a vehicle's rear window. These antennas consist of two parts: the outside antenna portion and the inside "base" portion, which is also glued to the window opposite the antenna.

Because these antennas couple the signal energy directly through the glass, there is no direct physical connection between the two parts. Although permanently mounted, the glass mount antenna requires no mounting holes and can be located near the vehicle's roof for better reception.

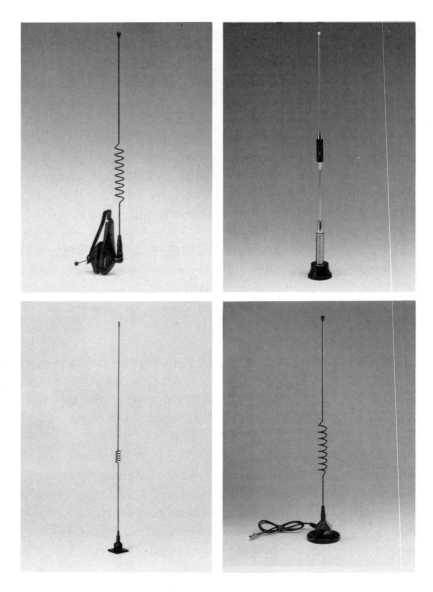

This page: *Mobile antennas (clockwise from top left); window mount, hole mount, magnetic mount, and glass mount.* (Courtesy Larsen Electronics, Inc.; glass mount courtesy Tandy Corp). Opposite page: *Grove model BRK9 Window Clip antenna bracket; permits external mounting of "rubber duckie" portable antennas for increased range. Includes two BNC connectors and several feet of feedline.* (Courtesy Grove Enterprises, Inc.)

Glass mount antennas have the same permanent mounting disadvantages as trunk lip and hole mount antennas. Since there is no direct electrical connection between antenna and feedline, some signal loss occurs in the coupling between the two parts.

Magnetic mount or "magmount" antennas are temporarily fastened to a vehicle with an integral magnetic base. These bases are designed to hold the antenna firmly in place at highway speeds. Normally, the bigger the mounting surface, the better the grip. On vehicles with a vinyl top, the antenna should be moved to the rear deck or trunk lid to ensure a good grip.

Magmounts offer the best of both worlds—easy portability and semi-permanent mounting. The only drawback is the difficulty in routing the feedline, as with gutter mount antennas.

If you don't want to add antennas to your car or if you're concerned about theft, vandalism, or suspicion, you can buy couplers that allow you to use your existing car radio antenna—or even your entire car chassis—as a scanner antenna.

These methods don't work quite as well as using dedicated scanner antennas, but offer the best possible solution for "stealth" monitoring. Fortunately, couplers don't interfere with regular AM/FM radio operation and performance.

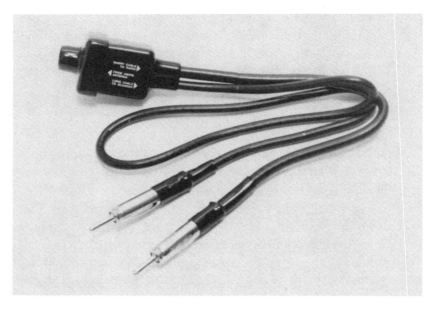

Para Dynamics model PDC-63 multicoupler; allows scanners to be used with car radio antennas; does not affect regular AM/FM reception. Both radios can be used simultaneously. (Courtesy Grove Enterprises, Inc.)

If you're into boating, you can connect your marine radio antenna to your scanner. VHF marine frequencies are in the range of 157 MHz, which is close enough to railroad frequencies to make marine antennas useful for monitoring railroad communications. Marine antennas can provide quite a lot of signal-pulling capability (up to 9dB) because they are often constructed by stacking antennas on top of each other (such as multiple quarter-wave whips), but this tends to make them very long—up to eight feet in length.

If you monitor at home, you can improve reception dramatically by using an outdoor roof-mounted antenna. If you live in a building with poor radio reception, an outdoor antenna can produce astonishing results. In some cases, you can triple or even quadruple your reception range. An outdoor base antenna can be used with bases, mobiles, and portables.

There are many types of outdoor antennas available; are all designed for broadband (wide frequency range) operation, so tuning and adjusting these antennas is neither recommended nor required. Outdoor base antennas all use integral ground planes, eliminating the need to create one.

To get the most out of your outdoor antenna, it must be positioned to intercept as many signals as possible. Since VHF radio waves travel in a line-of-sight fashion, this means getting the antenna as high as possible. On most homes, this means mounting the antenna on the roof. If this is impossible, base antennas can sometimes be erected in attics with sufficient vertical clearance and non-metallic roofs.

Base antennas are designed to be mounted with readily available television antenna mounting hardware (support masts, towers, tripods, chimney mounts, vent pipe mounts, etc.), which simplifies mounting tasks.

Grove model ANT-5 scanner antenna for rooftop, attic, and wall mounting; length, 68 inches; includes impedance transformer, horizontal offset pipe, and mounting hardware; mounts using standard TV antenna hardware. (Courtesy Grove Enterprises, Inc.)

Be careful when erecting rooftop antennas. Countless people have backed off roofs or have slipped and fallen with disastrous consequences. If you plan to do your own rooftop antenna installations, make sure you have the tools, skills, and assistance to do the job safely. You MUST read, follow, and understand the installation instructions and safety notices included with the antenna and mounting hardware!

If you are unsure about your abilities, it's a good idea to consult a professional before proceeding. If you're still unsure, let the pro do the job. To find an antenna installer, look in the yellow pages under "Antennas."

When doing an installation, you MUST make sure your antenna does not and cannot come in contact with any power lines before, during, and after installation. If an antenna falls onto or touches a live wire, you and anyone coming in contact with the antenna, feedline, or scanner could be KILLED or severely burned. Always assume overhead lines are live and carry lethal voltages. In addition to electrocution hazards, contact with live wires creates an explosive fire hazard that could burn your house down.

Even if your antenna is well clear of power lines, consider what would happen if the antenna were to fall to the ground. Would it fall into the street? Perhaps on a pedestrian? Would it crash through a window? Remember that calm weather conditions one day could turn into an antenna-wrenching storm the next.

The results of a lightning strike on improperly grounded antennas and radio gear can be devastating. Lightning can destroy radio gear and start fires, and if you're foolish enough to operate a scanner during a thunderstorm, electrocute or burn you. In addition, when lightning strikes an antenna, it typically energizes all wiring within the house including power, telephone, and cable TV. This can severely damage anything connected to these lines.

When using outdoor antennas, you MUST take steps to protect your home from lightning hazards. The antenna support mast must be grounded with an 8-gage conductor to a cold water pipe, an 8-foot copper ground rod driven into the earth, or both, per Section 810 of the National Electric Code.

The antenna feedline must be disconnected from your scanner and grounded whenever the scanner is not in use, especially when thunderstorms are in the area. A grounded coaxial switch automatically does this with a twist of a knob. Lightning arrestors, which are connected in series with the feedline, are also highly recommended because they automatically divert voltage surges to ground.

Keep in mind that a direct lightning strike is not needed to damage radio equipment. A powerful nearby strike can fill the air with enough energy to send a few hundred volts down the antenna feedline. Since lightning is just static electricity on a massive scale, an ungrounded, disconnected antenna can hold a weak lightning-induced charge for many hours. If a scanner is connected to a statically charged antenna, it can be damaged beyond repair.

Believe it or not, snow blowing across antennas at high rates of speed can also charge up antennas, an effect called "snow static." This charge can easily be large enough to damage a scanner. Again, make sure you ground all outdoor antennas whenever they're not in use to avoid problems.

If your outdoor antenna is installed safely, chances are you won't have any trouble. After all, millions of homes host television, ham, shortwave, and CB antennas without problems of any sort. Be careful and you won't become a statistic.

Feedline

Although it makes sense to mount an antenna as high as possible to maximize reception, this can be carried only so far. Unfortunately, as antenna height increases, so does the length of feedline needed to interconnect the scanner and antenna. This is a problem because long feedlines tend to absorb and weaken signals, especially at UHFs.

Fortunately, most railroad communications take place in the VHF region, which is not as susceptible to feedline loss as UHFs. To give you an idea of how much signal can be lost in a feedline at railroad frequencies, assume you are using high quality coaxial cable (such as type RG-8/U) to feed your scanner. If your feedline is 200 feet long, nearly half the signal voltage from the antenna will be lost.

If you use less expensive, smaller cable, like type RG-58/U, nearly three-quarters of the signal voltage will be lost. If you continue to increase the length of your feedline, you'll eventually reach a point where all of the signal will be lost, and you'd be much better off using the antenna supplied with the scanner.

As this example points out, it's a good idea to keep your feedline under 100 feet long and to use only high quality coaxial cable, such as RG-8/U. If you cannot avoid long feedline runs, or if you need to get your antenna up really high to receive signals effectively, a remote signal amplifier (discussed in the next section) can overcome feedline losses.

There are many ways to route the feedline to your indoor listening location. If you have attic vents, the feedline can be run through a vent and into the attic, thence down through a closet or wall to reach your scanner. You can also route the feedline through a foundation vent and into a cellar or crawlspace and then up through a floor. Less desirable entry methods include drilling through window casings, walls, and foundations. Sleeves are available for placement into these holes for easier routing of cables.

For mobile installations, it's a good idea to avoid pinching or crushing the feedline when routing through doors or windows, although this is often impossible. It's best to run the feedline into the vehicle compartment from the trunk via the back seat, and then along or under the door step plates to the front seat area.

Once the feedline has reached the scanner, a connector must be installed if not already attached. The easiest connector to install on coaxial cable is the PL-259, or UHF, connector. However, since many scanners accept the BNC connector, a PL-259-to-BNC adapter will be needed. BNC connectors are difficult and frustrating to install, even for experienced techs. Instructions for installing connectors are usually provided with the connector. For information on soldering, see *Building your own gear* in Chapter 6.

To connect a single feedline to multiple scanners, a multicoupler or coaxial switch should be used. A coaxial switch contains a rotary selector that connects one of several scanners to the antenna and usually includes an "off" position that disconnects and grounds the antenna for maximum lightning protection. A multicoupler is a signal splitter that "fans out" the signal from the antenna and isolates each output, thus allowing multiple scanners to be operated simultaneously.

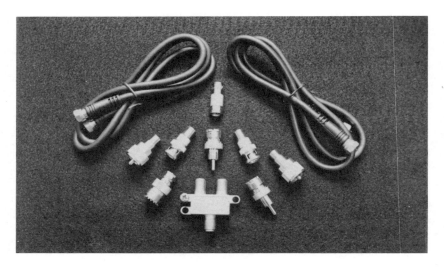

Grove model CPL-SC dual scanner multicoupler for connecting two scanners to a single antenna; includes adaptors for a variety of connector styles, and interconnecting cables. (Courtesy Grove Enterprises, Inc.)

Signal Amplifiers

Signal amplifiers are devices that boost the strength of radio signals entering your scanner. They are especially useful for overcoming signal losses caused by long feedline runs and for boosting the sensitivity of low and poor-sensitivity scanners (with or without outdoor antennas). Signal amplifiers can be used with all types of antennas and with all types of scanners.

Amplifiers can be both a curse and a blessing. If you monitor in an urban area and have a sensitive scanner or a scanner with an outdoor antenna with less than 100 feet of feedline, the amplifier may do more harm than good. It will overload your scanner and cause intermodulation interference *(see Chapter 4)*.

To combat intermodulation, some manufacturers market in-line feedline filters to suppress interfering signals. In addition, some amplifiers feature built-in interference filters and have provisions for adjusting the gain to a point where overload just begins to occur. Unfortunately, in many urban areas this point is zero and signal density is so great that filters are largely ineffective.

On the other hand, if you live in an urban area and have a long feedline or if you listen primarily in rural areas, an amplifier may improve reception dramatically. Rural areas tend to have fewer radio transmitters about, greatly reducing the chances of intermodulation.

Remember that an amplifier can't perform miracles—it simply can't make poor antennas or good antennas in poor locations receive signals. For instance, think of your antenna as a microphone and the signal amplifier as an audio amplifier. If the microphone is not picking up any sound, you can't expect the

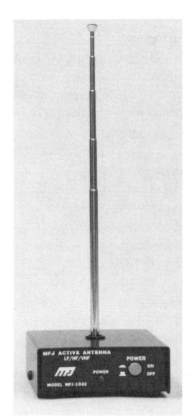

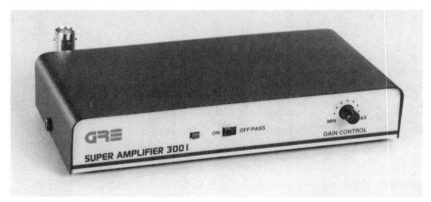

TL: *MFJ model 1022 active antenna with collapsible whip, 0.3–200 MHz coverage.* (Courtesy MFJ Enterprises, Inc). TR: *GRE in-line portable amplifier, 20dB gain, adjustable.* Bottom: *GRE model 3001 base amplifier, 20dB gain, adjustable; whip antenna available.* (GRE photos courtesy Tandy Corp.)

TL: *Grove model FTR6 Interference Eliminator; cuts interference from AM broadcast and and CB radio transmissions when monitoring VHF and UHF frequencies; installs in-line on antenna feedline; a similar model cuts interference from aircraft transmissions.* TR: *Grove model FTR5 Scanner Filter; cuts interference from FM broadcast, TV, aircraft, paging, and mobile telephone transmissions; installs in-line on antenna feedline; built-in notch filter is tunable from 100–220 MHz.* Bottom: *Grove model PRE5 Signal Booster; –10 to +18 dB attenuation/gain, adjustable; remote amplifier unit (on top of control box) is powered through the feedline and can be mounted anywhere on the feedline; can be mounted at or near the antenna to overcome feedline loss. A built-in multicoupler permits the connection of two scanners to the antenna.* (All photos courtesy Grove Enterprises, Inc.)

amplifier to which it's connected to generate any sound. If you increase the gain of the amplifier (turn it up), all you're going to hear is hiss and noise. It's the same with a signal amplifier. If there are no signals at your antenna, all the signal amplifier will do is amplify hiss and noise and, at the same time, introduce some noise of its own.

Likewise, for listeners using outdoor antennas, feedline losses can completely dissipate signals before they reach the scanner—making an amplifier connected at the scanner useless. This is why antenna-mounted (remote) amplifiers are used to combat feedline loss. A remote amplifier boosts signals when they're at their strongest and purest, i.e., at the antenna.

On the other hand, if you're not suffering from excessive feedline loss or if you have a good antenna, you can improve your scanner's sensitivity by installing an amplifier at the radio end of the feedline. Of course, portable users have no choice but to install a battery-operated amplifier directly at the antenna connector when using a portable antenna.

A combined antenna-amplifier unit called an active antenna is available for indoor use. These are ideal for listeners that cannot or do not want to erect an outdoor antenna. However, keep in mind that the amplifier cannot boost signals if they don't exist at the antenna.

If you decide to try a signal amplifier, remember that it may not work and may even make things worse. The only way to really know whether an amplifier is going to improve reception is to test it in actual service.

Amplifiers used at the radio are relatively simple to install and test. However, remote amplifiers are difficult to test because they must be installed at the antenna and consist of two parts: the remote amplifier and the indoor power unit. Fortunately, remote amplifiers are powered directly through the feedline, making extra wiring unnecessary, but the power unit must be connected to the feedline and an ac power source.

Another factor to consider when investigating signal amplifiers is noise. All amplifiers add a certain degree of undesirable noise, or hiss, to received signals, some more than others. You can get a good idea of an amplifier's noise performance by checking out its noise figure specs. Good performance is indicated by noise figures in the range of 3dB; as this figure increases, noise increases. Normally, the more expensive the amplifier, the better the noise performance.

Amplifier gain is also important because as gain increases, received signal strength increases. However, remember that increased gain is useful only if the amplifier has good noise specs and the gain does not overload the scanner.

To understand gain specifications, it's useful to know that a gain of 3dB is equivalent to increasing the power of the signal you're listening to by two times; 7dB by five times; 10dB by ten times; 13dB by 20 times; 17dB by 50 times; 20dB by 100 times; and 30dB by 1,000 times.

Professional Radio Equipment

Commercial, military, government, public safety, and industrial organizations—including railroads—typically use radio equipment designed for maximum performance under adverse operating conditions. This professional-level equipment is extremely rugged and reliable and offers excellent performance characteristics, especially in receive sensitivity, selectivity, and dynamic range.

Because professional equipment is often used in life-or-death situations, there can be no room for equipment shortcomings or failures. This high level of performance does not come cheap—professional gear can be up to ten times more expensive than consumer gear. However, good used professional gear can often be found at reasonable prices at electronics flea markets, as described in Chapter 6.

Ham radio gear offers a balance between consumer and professional equipment in both price and performance. Although not as rugged as professional equipment, ham radio transceivers and receivers offer excellent receive capabilities at a much lower relative cost. In addition, ham radio gear usually offers many useful "bells and whistles" such as frequency management functions not found on commercial equipment.

Since most professional equipment (except receivers and service monitors) can transmit as well as receive, you must be careful not to transmit with it except in life or death situations. Likewise, do not transmit with ham radio gear unless you're a licensed ham. Penalties for interfering with communications, whether intentional or not, are *extremely* severe due to the critical nature of most public safety and industrial communications. Federal law enforcement and regulatory agencies—and hams themselves—employ highly effective, sophisticated techniques to track down interfering signals.

Computer Interfaces

The mating of personal computers and scanners has given scanner listeners a new degree of power and flexibility. Users can scan thousands of channels at speeds exceeding 65 channels per second. In addition, more control is gained over standard scanner functions such as scan rate, delay, and lockout. For instance, scan rate and delay can be set at different speeds and times for specific channels or groups of channels.

Top: *Yaesu model FT-8500 VHF ham transceiver. Features include detachable remote front panel; "smart" speaker-microphone housing all radio controls; coded squelch capability; DTMF keypad; 110 memory channels; scanning; optional computer interface; 0.18 µV receive sensitivity (12dB SINAD); 60dB selectivity; 70dB intermodulation; VHF receive range, 110–174 MHz.* (Courtesy Yaesu U.S.A.)

Bottom: *Optoelectronics model 535 computer interface for computer-aided scanning; enables advanced search and logging capabilities including autologging with date and time stamp; DTMF tone decoding; digital and tone coded squelch capability. Shown with Radio Shack model PRO-2035 scanner; circuit card fits inside scanner chassis. Requires DOS-based computer and scan software such as ScanStar or ScanCat Gold.* (Courtesy Optoelectronics, Inc.)

Coded squelch techniques, such as tone (TPL™) and digital (DPL™), can be decoded to control scanner squelch functions *(see next section)*. Also, a programmable control output allows users to activate and deactivate a tape recorder according to a variety of parameters including frequency, time of day, squelch mode, etc.

Because frequencies are stored in computer memory, users can quickly generate a wide variety of reports on such things as channel activity, for example, how many times a channel was active and at what times. Automatic links to extensive FCC databases can be established to provide information on channel users, transmitter locations and power, distance from transmitters, etc.

Several manufacturers market a variety of scanner-to-computer interfaces that allow users to control scanner functions with off-the-shelf software packages.

Coded Squelch Decoders

Scanner users, just as railroaders, can use coded squelch techniques to avoid receiving unwanted transmissions *(see Chapter 2)*. Most high-end scanners and scanner-computer combinations can decode squelch signals, thus making it possible to select the kinds of communications you'd like to hear.

To use coded squelch techniques, the transmitted signal must carry a coded squelch signal. The easiest way to determine whether or not a signal is squelch-coded is with a decoder. Most off-the-shelf scanner-computer software packages include decoders that detect both TPL and DPL. Standalone decoder units are also available for detecting TPL and DPL codes.

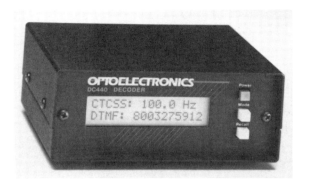

Optoelectronics model DC440 decoder; simultaneously reads DTMF tones and tone and digital coded squelch signals. (Courtesy Optoelectronics, Inc.)

TPL codes can be determined without a decoder, although not easily. To do so, you must enter all 42 tone frequencies into 42 channels of your scanner. Your frequency of interest must then be programmed into the 42 channels, and then all 42 channels monitored. If a transmission unsquelches your scanner, it is carrying a TPL code. To identify the code, simply note the channel and determine its corresponding PL code.

Voice-Activated Recorders

When you monitor events as they actually happen, you're listening in "real time." Conversely, when you monitor events that have already occurred, you're listening in "non-real time." This is similar to watching a live television broadcast versus watching a recorded daytime soap opera in the evening on a VCR.

By using similar taping methods and automatic voice activation, it's possible to monitor railroad communications in non-real time. This allows you to listen to a whole day's and night's worth of communications in just a few minutes, whenever you want to. You don't have to listen to the radio for 24 hours to hear everything.

The disadvantage is, of course, that you'll be listening to events that occurred earlier. However, for operations that take a long time with little contact with the dispatcher, such as a local freight switching a long, lightly used branchline, this isn't a limitation. You can check your recording to see if the local was given permission to enter the branch, eliminating hit-or-miss trips to observe the operation.

There are many recorders on the market today that facilitate non-real time monitoring. These recorders look and function very much like a standard portable cassette recorder, but are voice-activated. These recorders record only when a signal is present and shut down during quiet periods. Some recorders feature an extra slow recording speed that puts a huge volume of information onto a standard cassette tape. Adapters are also available to retrofit off-the-shelf recorders, and many external speaker-amplifier units contain voice-activated outputs for standard recorders.

One interesting application of the recorder is to use it as a train logger. If your home setup is within range of a RAD, it's possible to record the passing of every train throughout the day and night—and identify them if the crew responds with their train number or symbol. If the RAD announces train speed, direction, number of cars, time of day, etc., you'll have a complete record of operations. If your local RAD carries a coded squelch signal, you'll be able to block out all other transmissions, making it much easier to log train activity.

External Speakers and Audio Amplifiers

The audio quality and volume of any scanner can be improved by connecting it to an external speaker or audio amplifier. As discussed in Chapter 4, many scanners use small speakers and low power audio amplifiers that yield less-than-ideal sound quality.

Grove model SP-200A Sound Enhancer external speaker unit; includes built-in audio amplifier and speaker, bass/ treble controls, audio shaper, noise limiter, tape activator, and solid oak cabinet. (Courtesy Grove Enterprises, Inc.)

External speakers and walkman-type headphones can be connected to a scanner through its headphone jack. Some base and mobile scanners feature dedicated connections for external speakers that allow the simultaneous use of headphones. External speakers include lapel-mounted models (similar to the type used by the police) and boxes that clip to automobile visors or mount under the dash. Small hi-fi speakers can also be used when fitted with the proper connector.

In mobile scanning setups, external speakers can be temporarily placed outside the vehicle to allow listening away from the vehicle. In the same manner, a weatherproof horn speaker can be permanently mounted behind the car radiator grille.

For a maximum boost in audio volume and quality, an external amplifier-speaker combination must be used. For in-home use, a scanner's headphone jack can be connected to any unused stereo amplifier input except the magnetic phono input, which will overload and distort the amplifier. If the amplifier doesn't have a monaural switch, the scanner's sound will be heard from only one speaker. A Y-adapter connected to both the left and right inputs of the stereo will solve this problem. The scanner's volume will also have to be adjusted for best results. For portable or outdoor use, battery-powered portable amplifier-speaker combinations are available. These units can often be powered by the ac mains and vehicle electrical systems in addition to batteries.

Area Repeaters

As discussed in Chapter 2, a repeater is a device that retransmits radio signals in order to increase the effectiveness of a radio transceiver. The repeater principle can also be used to improve the effectiveness of any scanner when used at home or within a limited area, such as a swap meet.

When an outdoor antenna is used with a scanner, the scanner's portability is limited by the antenna feedline. To listen in other areas, it would be necessary to turn up the volume or install multiple extension speakers, which could be undesirable or impractical. By setting up an area repeater, it would be possible transmit the audio from a fixed scanner to any scanner within range.

Wireless room or baby monitors can be used as an area repeater by placing the transmitter unit next to the scanner's loudspeaker. Any audio from the scanner will be picked up by the transmitter and rebroadcast to the room monitor receiver or any scanner tuned to the correct frequency. Room monitors can have a surprisingly long range—up to a quarter-mile—depending upon the location of the transmitting unit and the receiver or scanner.

The transmit frequency of the room monitor is sometimes listed on a label affixed to the unit. If it's not, try the following frequencies: 49.830, 49.845, 49.860, 49.875, and 49.890 MHz. To find the frequency, play a radio station into the transmitter unit and listen for it on the scanner. If you don't hear it, use the search mode on the scanner, if so equipped, to search all frequencies between 46.500 and 47.500 MHz and 49.500 and 50.500 MHz. While searching, you'll probably hear many other room monitors, especially in urban areas.

FM wireless microphones can also be used as area repeaters, but are battery-powered and tend to go through batteries fairly quickly. Wireless mics usually transmit on standard FM broadcast frequencies, which are normally unavailable on most scanners, although some may use the 49 MHz band.

Drastic Measures

If you've tried all the reception-enhancing techniques to no avail, you may be too far away from your railroad of interest to hear anything, especially if you can receive signals from other services. However, if you are willing to experiment, you might be in range if you employ special antenna techniques in conjunction with the methods described previously.

Beam Antennas—Beam antennas are high-gain directional antennas. They differ from whips and ground plane antennas in one significant way: They are optimized to pick up signals from one direction only, whereas whips and ground planes are omnidirectional—they pick up signals equally at all points of the compass. Although beams are directional, they can still receive signals from other directions.

Because they concentrate reception, beams are true gain antennas. Whips and ground planes are not; they exhibit gain only because it's impossible not to. This is because gain is measured relative to an ideal isotropic antenna that cannot be achieved in actual practice.

When it comes to gain, the designed-for-gain beam is a hands down winner. Large beam antennas have gains approaching 15dB (equivalent to multiplying transmitter power 30 times), whereas the best whips and ground planes only have gains of around 3dB (doubles transmitter power).

Because of the beam's concentrated pickup pattern, it must be pointed in the direction of the transmitter you'd like to hear, like an outdoor TV antenna, which is actually a high-gain, wideband beam. For example, if you live south of an east-west railroad, you'd point the antenna NW to NE to monitor the railroad's communications. If you wish to monitor multiple railroads located around the compass, a TV antenna rotator can be used to aim the antenna in the proper directions.

If you decide to use a beam, you can purchase a professional-grade antenna, which like professional radio equipment, is very durable and therefore very expensive. Alternatively, you can purchase a consumer-grade beam that offers professional performance with less durability for a much lower price.

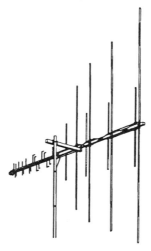

Grove Scanner Beam; 6–9dB gain, 30–960 MHz, vertically polarized; can be permanently aimed in the direction of desired signals or rotated as needed with an ordinary TV antenna rotor. (Courtesy Grove Enterprises, Inc.)

Towers—Raising your antenna higher into the air always increases signal pickup because the antenna is more in the transmitting antenna's line of sight. However, as discussed previously, raising the antenna also increases the length of the feedline, which results in increased feedline loss. If you use a tower (you can easily raise your antenna 50 feet), you will definitely have to use a remote signal amplifier to overcome loss.

There are two main types of towers available, self-supporting and guyed. Self-supporters do not require guy lines, which tend to get in the way and take up a lot of space on the ground. However, they are heavily constructed and cost a lot more than guyed towers, which use lighter construction.

Both types of towers are available in crank-up form, where the mid-section of the tower is hinged to allow the upper portion to be raised and lowered with a crank-and-cable mechanism. Raising and lowering the tower from the ground eliminates the need to climb when maintaining or replacing antennas.

Erecting a tower is definitely not a job for the inexperienced. Numerous things can go wrong that can result in serious personal injury or DEATH. All of the warnings and conditions that apply to installing rooftop antennas applies doubly so for towers. Unless you've had previous experience in erecting towers, leave the job to a pro. Look in the yellow pages under "Antennas" to find a qualified tower erection specialist.

Be aware that towers are not welcomed in many areas, especially planned "bedroom" communities. Some enforce statutes that prohibit or limit large antennas and towers. While ham radio operators have successfully challenged these limitations, some have paid the price; they've endured threats of physical violence, vandalism, and in a few cases, towers have been pulled down.

Thus, make sure you check the zoning bylaws in your area before you install a tower. If you live close to an airport, you may also need approval from the Federal Aviation Administration or Transport Canada. If you don't plan properly, you may end up having to dismantle your antenna, or worse yet, face the wrath of the "nimbies."

Passive repeaters—If a large hill stands between your home and the railroad you'd like to monitor, you've definitely got a line-of-sight problem. If the hill is directly behind your house and you own the land or can get permission to use the land, you could use the hill like a tower. You could set up your beam on the hill and point it toward the railroad. However, this could become impractical due to long feedline requirements and the need to place amplifiers along the line.

The use of multiple amplifiers is problematic because there are no easy ways to power any amplifiers beyond the one closest to the home. These amplifiers would require the running of a separate all-weather ac line along the cable and the use of weatherproof power boxes, with concomitant astronomical costs. Battery-powered amplifiers would be more practical, but would require constant maintenance.

In lieu of cables, a passive repeater can be used to direct radio signals toward your home. As discussed in Chapter 2, a passive repeater consists of two electrically-connected antennas placed back-to-back. One antenna would be pointed toward the railroad, with the other pointed toward your scanner antenna, effectively replacing the hard-wire link with radio. To minimize signal losses, all three antennas must be carefully aimed and the feedline linking the two repeating antennas kept as short as possible.

CHAPTER 6

Scanning on a Budget

Fortunately, for those on tight budgets, a high-performance listening setup can be assembled for very little money. Contrary to popular belief, there are many ways to get excellent performance "on the cheap." These include buying used gear, using existing antennas, and building your own antennas.

The popularity of cable television, the decline of CB radio, the demise of crystal-controlled scanners, and general advancements in technology have created a large surplus of of used radio and antenna gear. A lot of this unwanted equipment was excellent in its time, and if well taken care of, can provide satisfactory performance at little or no cost.

The classifieds in local newspapers and national radio magazines almost always have ads for used scanners, antennas, and related accessories *(see Appendix G)*. Tag sales and auctions are also good sources for used gear at good prices. Perhaps the greatest source of all time is the hamfest, a party-like gathering of ham radio operators. One of the biggest and most popular events at a hamfest is the flea market.

Flea markets are loaded with all kinds of deals for the bargain hunter. You can find feedline, antennas, antenna hardware, towers, and most importantly—scanners, receivers, service monitors, ham radio transceivers, and other professional gear.

Hamfests are held year round all over the U.S. and Canada, but more so in the summer. You can find out about hamfests in your area by checking out the listings in the radio hobby magazines or by sending a SASE to the American Radio Relay League, 225 Main St., Newington, Conn. 06111.

Finally, discarded coaxial cable, antenna masts, rotors, etc. from abandoned CB and TV antenna setups can often be found in impromptu dumps along the tracks. These materials are often in serviceable condition, especially the coaxial cable, and the price is right.

Buying used gear can be a gamble because most transactions are made on a where-is, as-is basis. If the equipment doesn't work, you're probably stuck with it. However, if it does work, you can get some truly good deals. Before buying used gear, try to determine whether it's in good working order. Ask for a demonstration before you buy. If this is not possible, discuss the possibility of getting your money back if it doesn't work. However, if the seller reneges on a deal, there's probably not much you can do about it.

Visual inspections of used gear are useful only in cases of extreme physical damage. Sometimes the worst-looking gear ends up working fine, while like-new equipment is completely shot. Without a demonstration, there's often no way to tell.

However, if coaxial cable is gouged, cracked, burned, crushed, or missing insulation—even slightly—it's best to leave it unless you can cut out the damaged sections and use the remainder. Unlike many items, the integrity of coaxial cable that otherwise looks fine can be easily tested by checking for shorts and opens (breaks) in the cable's conductors.

To check for shorts, make sure the cable's center conductor and outside mesh braid aren't touching each other at both ends of the cable. At one end, probe the center conductor and the outside mesh simultaneously with an ohmmeter. If the meter deflects, the cable is shorted and should not be used. To check for opens (after checking for shorts), short the cable's center conductor and outside mesh at one end only. Probe the center conductor and mesh at the opposite end. If the meter does not deflect, the cable is open and should not be used.

Finally, remember that prices vary quite widely on the used market. Shop around and don't hesitate to bargain, especially at hamfests later in the day—everyone becomes anxious to unload the "junk."

The Used Equipment Market

At the upper end of the market you'll find programmable scanners in all configurations, newer antennas, and professional-level radios. At the lower end, you'll find plenty of older antennas, feedline, VHF tuners, and crystal-controlled scanners and receivers.

Many CB and VHF ham radio antennas can be modified to work as excellent scanner antennas. Whip antennas without coils can be trimmed and tuned to work at railroad frequencies as described in Chapter 5. Likewise, ground plane antennas can be similarly tuned, except that all elements (vertical and horizontal) should be trimmed to the same length. Of course, used scanner antennas can be similarly tuned.

Outdoor TV antennas, which are actually wideband beams, make excellent scanner antennas when they're polarized properly. Polarization is simply how the antenna is situated in relation to the horizon. If an antenna is oriented parallel to the horizon, like most outdoor TV antennas, it's horizontally po-

The author's fixed field antenna, an old CB ground plane trimmed to the railroad band. Support is a ten-foot length of banister stock. Extreme caution is always taken to avoid contacting the antenna with power and signal lines.

larized. If it's perpendicular to the horizon, like a whip antenna, it's vertically polarized.

Transmitting and receiving antennas must share the same polarization for maximum signal transfer, otherwise up to 20dB of signal can be lost—equivalent to the transmitter reducing its power by 100 times. Since railroad transmitting antennas are vertically polarized, receiving antennas must be vertically polarized as well. Therefore, TV antennas must be flipped 90 degrees and remounted so the elements are perpendicular to the horizon.

Indoor TV antennas such as rabbit ears can also be used as scanner antennas, and their telescoping elements are ideal for tuning. Some indoor antennas have built-in amplifiers; these make excellent indoor active antennas. However, you'll have to match the 300 ohm twinlead output to your scanner input. This can be done with a 300-to-75 ohm cable TV matching transformer and an adapter to convert the transformer's F-style connector to one that mates with your scanner.

If you have a CB or TV antenna on your roof and don't wish to modify it, connect it to your scanner anyway. If your built-in scanner antenna isn't working well, you have nothing to lose; the existing antenna could work surprisingly well. Remember that you may have to use adapters to make the connections.

As a result of the meteoric rise and fall of CB radio, feedline is plentiful—and very reasonably priced—on the used market. Furthermore, many CB installations were wired with low-loss RG-8/U coaxial cable, making it widely available. Many other types of coaxial cable can also be found. The *Radio Amateur's Handbook*, published by the American Radio Relay League, lists the more common varieties along with loss specifications.

As discussed previously, you should use cable with the lowest loss unless you are using a signal amplifier or your feedline is relatively short—under 50 feet or so. In addition to standard 52 ohm radio cable, 75 ohm video cable such as type RG-59/U will yield excellent results when used with a scanner. Instructions for attaching connectors to cables are usually supplied with the connector. If not, instructions can be found in the *Radio Amateur's Handbook*.

In the late seventies, advancements in microprocessor technology ushered in a new wave of scanners in which users could select and store frequencies into scores of channels using a touch keypad. Previously, frequencies were determined by small, plug-in modules called crystals, so named because they contain a small slice of quartz cut to vibrate at the frequency of operation. Because one crystal was required for each operating frequency, crystal expenses (around $5.00 per channel) limited most scanners to 20 channels or less.

A variation of the crystal scanner was the service monitor, which was used to monitor one or two channels continually. Frequencies were selected with a front-panel switch.

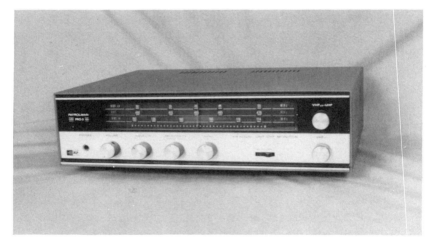

Top: *Craig model 4350A VHF–UHF base/mobil scanner; crystal-controlled, 120 Vac or 12 Vdc operation; all-metal construction; scans even when receiver is unsquelched. Hamfest purchase, $3.00; an identical unit was purchased at another hamfest for a dollar. This unit is used in conjunction with the setup pictured on page 124.*

Bottom: *Realistic Patrolman PRO-3 VHF–UHF base/mobil tuner; 120 Vac or 12 Vdc operation; all-metal construction; built-in loudspeaker; switchable 5 or 15 kHz selectivity; hiss filter. Hamfest purchase, $15.00. Styled to match the DX-160 HF shortwave receiver.*

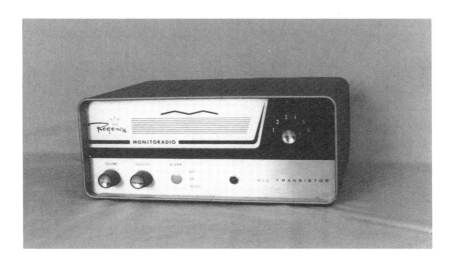

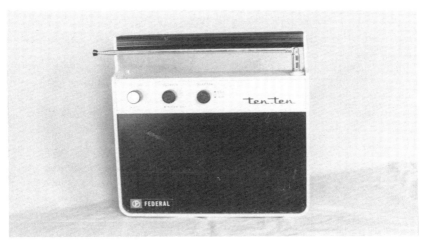

Top: *Regency model TMH2 "all transistor" service monitor; six channels, selectable; 120 Vac or 12 Vdc operation; all-metal construction; built-in loudspeaker. Note that "alarm" option was not supplied with this model; this function would respond to the same tones that activate sirens at fire stations (recall the two tones that would precede the alarm on the 70s action show,* Emergency). *The radio would emit an alarm tone in response to the signal. This radio was obtained for free; it was being discarded by a local AM radio station.*

Bottom: *Federal model Ten-Ten portable service monitor; 120 Vac or 12 Vdc operation; ruggedized all-metal construction; built-in loudspeaker and antenna; includes alarm function. Professional-level. Hamfest purchase, one dollar.*

The convenience and flexibility of programmable scanners quickly doomed "rockbound" crystal-controlled scanners. For those on a budget, crystal scanners in excellent condition can be had for a few dollars. Crystal costs can be minimized by monitoring only one or two important frequencies or by acquiring crystals from an old-time railfan.

Another disadvantage of many crystal scanners is their inability to function at railroad VHF frequencies. Because many of these units were designed for police and fire listening, they were optimized for frequencies around 155 MHz. This doesn't seem too far away from 160 MHz railroad frequencies, but in those days, designing a scanner to tune a wide range of frequencies was difficult and expensive.

Fortunately, tuning ranges are often listed on the back or bottom of the scanner, such as, "VHF hi 152–160" or "155." In the first example, the scanner is designed to work well within these frequency limits and perhaps a bit outside as well. In the second, the scanner is designed to work on frequencies right around 155 MHz, i.e., 154–156 MHz.

As the name implies, tuners receive a broad range of frequencies, much like a standard AM/FM radio. They were popular in the old days because they could tune a broad range of frequencies, unlike their contemporary crystal scanners. The programmable scanner's wide frequency range quickly killed the demand for tuners.

Of course, the biggest drawback of a tuner is that it doesn't scan. However, they are still useful because they can be permanently set to a receive a single, active frequency such as a road channel. However, finding a frequency can be very frustrating because tuners use analogue "slide rule" tuning, not a digital readout. To complicate matters, railroad frequencies can be quiet for long intervals.

The best way to tune a railroad frequency is to use the National Weather Service broadcasts as a guide. Since NWS forecasts are transmitted continuously near 162.5 MHz, the accuracy of the tuning dial can be checked and a good guess made as to where to tune for the desired frequency.

To increase your chances of finding a frequency, borrow a scanner and monitor your frequency of interest. When you hear a transmission on the scanner, quickly adjust the tuning back and forth on the tuner until you hear the signal. Once you locate the frequency, put an identifying mark on the tuning dial in case you accidently knock it off frequency.

Building Your Own Gear

By "homebrewing" equipment, you can save money while learning about radio electronics. For starters, you could build your own antennas and power cables. For more advanced projects, plans and complete kits are available for antennas, receivers, wireless microphones, power supplies, filters, frequency counters, converters, amplifiers, etc. *(see Appendix G)*.

Although the following projects don't require a knowledge of electronics, numerous books, magazines, and videos are available to give beginners a good grasp of basic electronics principles and construction techniques.

Most electronics projects require soldering. You can learn to solder by practicing "dry runs" on scrap pieces of wire and cable. The important things to remember about soldering are:

- To solder antenna wire, you'll need quite a lot of heat; a 100 watt solder gun will do a good job. For smaller wires, use a lower-wattage soldering iron.
- Steel and aluminum can't be soldered—copper and nickel (solid or plated) solder very well.

- Dirty, tarnished surfaces can't be easily soldered, they should be cleaned with steel wool or emery cloth before soldering.
- Don't use acid core plumbing solder; use rosin core electronics solder.
- A strong mechanical joint solders much better than a loose one.
- Heat the joint to be soldered and apply solder directly to the joint, not to the gun or iron.
- Continue to heat the joint until the solder freely flows all around it. Don't move it until the solder solidifies.
- Heat the joint only enough to flow the solder. Otherwise, insulation may melt off wires or other burning could occur.
- A good solder connection appears smooth and shiny—a poor one appears rough, cakey, and dull.
- If necessary, reheat the joint and add or reflow the solder to obtain a good connection.
- Wires conduct and retain heat; beware of burns!

Antenna and power cables can be constructed fairly easily. Wire, connectors (antenna, cigarette lighter, power, etc.), and solder are inexpensive and widely available from local electronics stores, flea markets, and catalogues. When wiring connectors, be careful not to reverse the connections; equipment won't work and could be severely damaged. Also, avoid applying too much heat when soldering, especially when working with smaller connectors and cables—shorts or burning could occur. Be sure to check for shorts with an ohmmeter. Instructions for wiring connectors are usually supplied with the connector.

The SO-239 quarter-wave ground plane antenna, long a ham favorite, is very easy to build and offers good performance for its size and simplicity. Although somewhat fragile, it offers good service when permanently mounted indoors in elevated places such as attics.

The heart of the antenna is the SO-239, or female UHF connector, the feedline receptacle found on most CB and ham sets and some scanners. The antenna elements—the vertical "hot" element and four horizontal ground plane radials—are attached directly to the connector.

The antenna is fed with standard coaxial cable and can be suspended from ceiling hooks or rafters with fishing line or twine. Metallic lines can degrade antenna performance.

To build the antenna, you'll need 10 feet of 10 to 14 gage solid copper wire, a silver- or nickel-plated SO-239 connector (for solderability), four 4-40 x 1/4 inch bolts and associated nuts/flatwashers, rosin core solder, an ohmmeter to check for shorts, and enough feedline to reach your listening location. If feedline connectors are not preattached, you'll need a connector to mate with your scanner. On long feedline runs, an amplifier may be required. These items can be purchased at local electronics stores, flea markets, and from catalogues.

Copper wire can also be salvaged from old house wiring or other abandoned lines. The wire can be either insulated or bare, it makes no difference as far as antenna performance is concerned. For tools you'll need a pair of wire cutters, needle nose pliers, wire strippers, utility knife, soldering gun, tape measure, screwdrivers, small wrench set, and an ohmmeter.

After you've identified a good location for your antenna and have all required materials, you'll need to calculate the element length for your frequency of interest. The length of each element—the main vertical element and the four radials—can be calculated using the formula given in Chapter 5.

Once you've determined the required length, cut five pieces of copper wire to this length plus roughly three inches. If insulated, remove several inches of insulation from the wires for soldering. These are the elements. Seat one element into the SO-239 center pin "stovepipe" opposite the threaded side and solder into place. For best results, hold the solder gun on the side of the stovepipe and flow the solder around the element and down into the pipe. Allow the connection to cool and solidify before moving anything.

Next, place four mounting bolts into the mounting holes on the SO-239 with the bolt heads opposite the stovepipe side. Install the washers and thread the bolts loosely. Using the needle nose pliers, bend one end of the remaining elements tightly around and under each washer, one element per bolt, and then tighten the nuts. At this point, you should have an SO-239 connector with one element soldered into the center stovepipe and four radials bolted down at each corner.

The next step is to cut the radials to the calculated length. To do so, measure from the edge of the connector. For the vertical element, measure from the bottom of the stovepipe, but leave an extra half-inch or so at the top. This allows you to bend a hook into the top of the element for easier hanging with the fishline. When making the bend, measure to the top of the bend to maintain proper element length.

The final step is to solder the radials to the SO-239 to ensure a good connection and to keep the nuts from loosening. With the nuts and bolts in place, apply plenty of heat to the bolts while flowing the solder around the heads, around the radials, under the nuts, and onto the connector surface. Be careful not to burn any work surfaces supporting the connector or radials. Allow the joints to cool and solidify before moving anything to avoid creating poor solder connections.

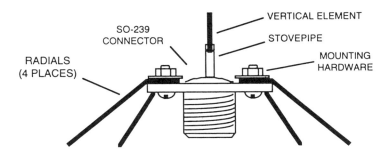

Close-up view of completed SO-239 antenna. Radials can be bent down at a 45-degree angle to obtain a better match to 52 ohm coaxial feedline. Not drawn to scale; mounting hardware is shown unsoldered.

The feedline is conveniently attached to the antenna directly through the SO-239 connector. A PL-259 connector is needed to mate with the SO-239. If not preattached, one can be installed following the instructions supplied with the connector. If a different connector is preattached, such as a BNC, an adapter can be used to make the connection.

At the scanner end of the feedline, a connector may need to be attached. The easiest one to install on coax cable is the PL-259. However, since many scanners accept the BNC connector, a PL-259–to–BNC adapter will be needed. BNCs are difficult and frustrating to install, even for experienced techs.

When soldering connectors, remember to avoid overheating the feedline. Use only enough heat to do the job and no more. Be sure to check for shorts using the ohmmeter. If any are found, cut back the feedline and reinstall the connector. If the connector can't be easily removed, use a new one.

The half-wave dipole is another simple, inexpensive antenna that works quite well, making it one of the most popular outdoor antennas of all time. Normally, dipoles are horizontally polarized, but their short length at VHF permits vertical mounting and polarization *(see page 138).*

The antenna consists of two quarter-wave elements placed end-to-end. One quarter-wave is "hot" while the other acts as a ground. The antenna is fed with standard coaxial cable and can stretched vertically between any two fixed points at least four feet apart for permanent mounting.

To build a dipole, you'll need around eight feet of 10 to 14 gage copper wire, three small spool or "dogbone" insulators, some sort of waterproof sealant, such as RTV silicon, rosin core solder, and enough feedline to reach your listening location. If feedline connectors are not preattached, you'll need a connector to mate with your scanner. On long feedline runs, an amplifier may be required. These items can be purchased from local electronics stores, flea markets, and catalogues.

Alternatively, copper wire can be salvaged from old house wiring or other abandoned lines. Small spool insulators can often be found on the ground along rail lines or on old electric fences. The wire can be either insulated or bare, it makes no difference as far as antenna performance is concerned.

For tools you'll need a pair of wire cutters, wire strippers, utility knife, pliers, soldering gun, tape measure, small screwdriver, and an ohmmeter.

After you've identified or constructed a good mounting location for your antenna and have all required materials, you'll need to calculate the antenna length for your frequency of interest. The length of each element (a single quarter wave) can be calculated using the formula given in Chapter 5.

Once you've determined the length, the next step is to construct the elements. First, cut your eight-foot length of wire in half. Take one wire and bend about eight inches of wire around (or through a hole of) an insulator. Wrap the wire tightly back around itself three or four times; it's best to keep the wraps closely spaced. Use a pair of pliers if necessary. Cut off excess wrap. Repeat the procedure for the remaining wire using another insulator. At this point you should have two wires with an insulator securely attached to one end of each.

Next, stretch one wire assembly out along the ground, and tie the insulator off to hold the assembly firmly in place when it's stretched. Bend the free end of the wire around (or through) the third insulator, but do not wrap. Place the end of the tape measure at the extreme end of the wire where the insulator is attached, i.e., at the far end of the loop at the insulator.

While stretching the wire taught, measure the element length per your calculations. Adjust the position of the unattached, free-end insulator until you achieve the desired length; again, make sure you measure to the extreme ends of the wire.

Double check all measurements and wrap the wire around the remaining insulator, making sure you maintain proper length. Cut off any excess wrap. At this point, you should have a piece of wire with an insulator attached at both ends. This is one element. When measured from extreme end to extreme end, the length should agree with your calculations.

The other element is constructed in the same manner as the first except the free end is attached to one of the insulators on the completed element. Remember to double check all measurements. When finished, you should have two elements of equal length joined by a center insulator, with insulators at each end. This is a half-wave dipole antenna.

To connect the feedline to the antenna, first remove any pre-attached connectors as necessary and about three inches of outer jacket from the coaxial cable. The easiest way to do this is with a multiple gage wire stripper. However, a utility knife can be used as long as the mesh immediately below the outer jacket is not nicked or damaged.

Once the outer jacket has been removed, carefully unbraid the wire mesh by combing it out with a small screwdriver or similar tool. The unbraided mesh is then twisted together to form a single "pig-tail" for connection to the antenna.

Next, remove about an inch of insulation from the feedline center conductor with the wire strippers. This can also be done with the utility knife if you take care not to nick the conductor. If insulated wires were used to construct the antenna, remove about three inches of insulation from both wires at the center insulator, as close as possible to the wrap.

Tightly wrap the prepared feedline conductors around the antenna elements, one conductor per element. Again, if you're using insulated wire, you'll have to remove some insulation to make the connections. Keep the connections as close as possible to the center insulator.

Solder the connections, taking care not to melt the feedline insulation, particularly the center conductor. Remember to allow each connection to cool and completely solidify before moving anything, otherwise a poor connection will result.

Once things have cooled off, check the solder connections to make sure you've got a good, bright, smooth solder joint. If not, reheat the connection and add solder as necessary. Put an ohmmeter across the elements to check for shorts. If the feedline is shorted, make sure the center conductor and braid aren't touching or shorted at the other end of the cable. If they aren't, cut the cable back at least two inches and reconnect per the previous instructions and recheck for shorts.

To keep water from entering the feedline and degrading antenna performance, apply silicon RTV sealant at the point where the center conductor and braid leave the feedline. Once the sealant cures, the antenna is ready for installation.

When installing the antenna, make sure the "hot" antenna element—the one connected to the feedline center conductor—is positioned on top. When the lines used to support the antenna, i.e., those attached to the end insulators, are more than six inches long, use nylon rope, not wire. Longer lengths could interfere with antenna operation and degrade performance.

Try to keep the feedline perpendicular (horizontal) to the antenna at the connection point. The feedline should also be securely attached to a stable anchoring point to minimize wind movement, which could eventually weaken and break the feedline connections.

Finally, when soldering connectors to the feedline, remember to avoid overheating. Use only enough heat to do the job and no more. Be sure to check for shorts. If any are found, cut back the feedline and reinstall the connector. If the connector can't be easily removed, use a new one.

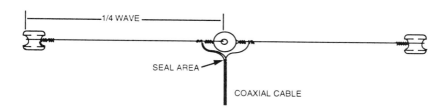

Completed half-wave dipole antenna; consists of two quarter-wave elements placed end-to-end and separated by an insulator. The point at which the conductors leave the coaxial feedline should be sealed with RTV silicone sealant to keep moisture from entering the feedline. Moisture can seriously degrade performance. "Dogbone" antenna insulators can be used, but old electric fence lines often yield spool insulators tor the taking. See the following page for recommended installation. Not drawn to scale.

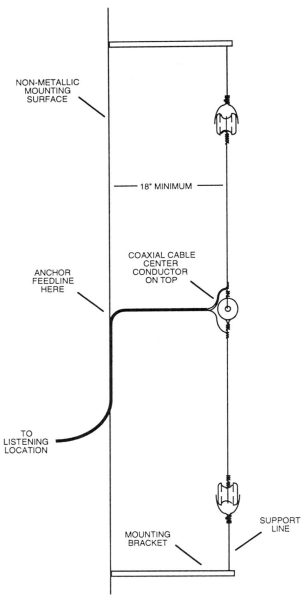

Half-wave dipole installation; support lines exceeding six inches should be non-metallic, e.g., nylon rope. Metallic mounting brackets may be used as long as they are kept perpendicular to the antenna. The feedline should also be kept perpendicular to the antenna at the feed point and must be anchored to reinforce the antenna connections. Not drawn to scale.

CHAPTER 7

The Future of Railroad Radio

Spectrum Congestion

The biggest immediate challenge facing railroad radio is spectrum congestion. Because many of today's growing communication technologies depend upon radio, there is constant pressure on federal agencies to free up channels. Since the Railroad Radio Service controls a big chunk of the radio spectrum, railroads are always under fire to spread the wealth.

Over the years, industry-backed pressure groups have lobbied to move railroads out of the VHF region. The railroads' neighbor in the spectrum, maritime radio, has continually pressed for railroads to move to UHF. The railroads have always resisted the change, citing costs and service interruptions.

However, with available frequencies dwindling at all points in the spectrum—both VHF and UHF—the FCC and Industry Canada have looked for ways to use the existing spectrum more efficiently. Along with narrowing bandwidths to 12.5 kHz (and eventually to 6.25 kHz), one of the biggest moves towards this end has been the implementation of trunked radio systems, particularly in the law enforcement community. The success of these systems makes it clear that all users, including railroads, will eventually adopt trunked technology.

Trunked radio systems operate on a shared-channel principle, much like the cellular telephone network. Because channels are shared by many users and allocated by computer, tremendous efficiencies can be realized. Communications that once consumed hundreds of channels can be conducted on as few as twenty-five.

A typical trunked radio system consists of multiple repeater sites, each capable of operating on the same frequencies, usually in the 800 or 900 MHz range. All sites are linked to a common computer-based control center using point-to-point microwave or landline links.

The control center sends supervisory information—information used to control transmit and receive functions at the repeater sites and at individual radios—via one of the communication channels. This channel is called the control channel and can be on a dedicated frequency or assigned at random by the computer. When a user presses the transmit switch on his radio, a request for channel command is sent to the control center via the control channel. The command includes digital information on the identity of the radio and the group to which the user belongs—maintenance, train crew, yard operations, etc.

The control center uses a voting function to select the repeater currently providing the best reception. If the reception deteriorates, another repeater is automatically selected to maintain optimum reception.

When a signal is received, the control center first determines whether the radio is authorized to access the trunked system.

If it is, the requesting radio is identified and the user's group is determined. The computer then searches for a clear channel and automatically assigns one to the user. At the same time, all radios within the operator's group are also switched to the same frequency so they can hear the call and respond if necessary. All this activity takes place in less than a second.

Some railroads, especially shortlines, have followed a trunked approach by using the public cellular telephone network. Ordinary cellphones are assigned to operating and maintenance crews, and all communications are conducted via telephone. In many cases, written orders and instructions are faxed to crews via field-ruggedized portable facsimile units.

New Applications

The resurgence of the railroad industry has allowed railroad companies to investigate, develop, and adopt leading-edge communications equipment and technologies. As a result of these actions, railroads have further reduced operating expenses and have enjoyed an even greater increase in revenues, return on investment, customer satisfaction, and profits.

To ensure future growth, railroads have continued to invest in research and development programs that underscore the importance of radio in all aspects of operations and maintenance. Companies such as CP Rail, Canadian National, Burlington Northern Santa Fe, Union Pacific, Southern Pacific, MTA, and BART have formed alliances with leading suppliers—Harmon, GE, Harris, Amtech, Rockwell, Electro-Motive, GRS, US&S, Hughes, et al.—to develop, test, and implement a variety of high-tech solutions that include critical radio operations.

Perhaps the most important future application for radio will be in automatic train control (ATC). These command and control systems will combine positioning technology, telemetry, and computer-assisted dispatching to increase train density. Trains will be able to run much faster and on much shorter headways. As ATC systems become more sophisticated, full remote control of trains will become possible, obviating the need for crews on terminal-to-terminal runs. Eventually, even locals and yard trains will run without crews as technology catches up with the tasks of remotely switching cars.

Future maintenance operations (and ATC systems) will rely heavily on radio-based equipment status and tracking. Telemetric links will join real-time, on-board monitoring systems with computers in dispatching and maintenance centers to detect such things as pending engine failures and low supply inventories. It will then be possible to maximize equipment usage and optimize inventory counts by tailoring maintenance and restocking schedules to meet the needs of individual pieces of equipment. Dispatchers will be able to anticipate problems and deal with them before they get out of hand.

As computer system implementation and technology move farther in the direction of shared data, radio will provide the links to join computer databases and CPUs across the rail network. These shared systems, combined with advanced ATC, will automate and decentralize train control to the point where even the traditional train dispatcher's responsibilities will become redundant.

Listening In

Unfortunately for railfans, future rail communication systems will bring an end to monitoring as it exists today. As railroads move to cellular/trunked operations in the 800 and 900 MHz bands, frequency assignments for specific operations will no longer exist, making it impossible to selectively monitor the different aspects of rail operations. It is also quite possible that rail frequencies could be shared with any number of other services, such as maritime radio, further reducing exclusivity.

Furthermore, the nature of trunked operations makes it difficult to monitor conversations because they can move from frequency to frequency without warning. All one can do is attempt to follow the conversation by continually hitting the scan button. To complicate matters, the supervisory information, which is transmitted in the form of very annoying trunking tones, can be transmitted on any system frequency at any time, making it impossible to lock out the tones.

Data communications will also become more prevalent as dispatchers and train crews send more and more of their messages via faxes and computer, much like our present day e-mail. As data communications become more prevalent, voice communications will dwindle, especially on road trains. Voice will be used to a greater extent on locals, in yards, and at maintenance facilities, but even these communications will be converted to digital modes that can't be heard with an ordinary scanner.

Even if digital-to-voice converters and data displays could be obtained, digital modes cannot be easily unscrambled. Without the proper "key," which can be changed several times an hour or more, it is for all practical purposes impossible to monitor scrambled communications, even with sophisticated decoding software. Even the brightest hackers would be humiliated and would risk arrest since the ECPA makes decoding communications unlawful.

Eventually, all railroad operations will become 100% computer-controlled with minimal human intervention—and therefore minimal voice communications.

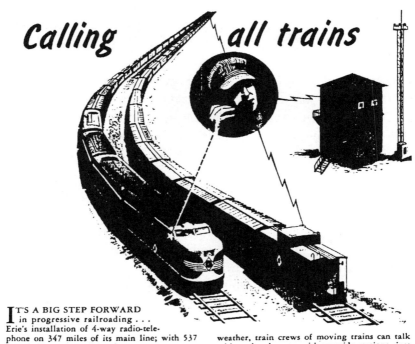

IT'S A BIG STEP FORWARD in progressive railroading... Erie's installation of 4-way radio-telephone on 347 miles of its main line; with 537 more miles soon to be under way.

Traditional methods, such as hand signals and walking the tracks now give way to the *instant* communication of radio-telephone. With radio, Erie conductors can talk to the engineer (and vice versa) *while the train is in motion.* In any weather, train crews of moving trains can talk with each other, or with wayside stations, just as easily as you use *your* telephone at home!

Read all about this newest phase of railroad communication in Erie's new folder "Calling All Trains at 50 Miles an Hour". Mail the coupon now for your free copy.

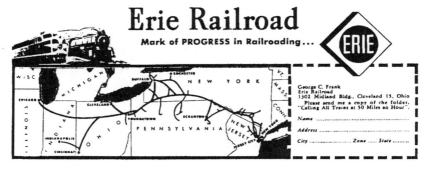

The Erie extols the virtues of its new "4-way radio-telephone" system in 1948. Yes, you could actually communicate with moving trains—with instant communication! Someday, perhaps in the not-so-distant future, the advertising of today will appear equally as quaint, if not more so. (Courtesy Lee Burbage)

APPENDIX A

Selected Railroad Radio Frequencies

The following frequencies cover road (train–dispatcher) or yard operations. Because of the popularity of programmable scanners, it should be possible to enter all frequencies for your railroad of interest. The content of the communications will identify their use.

Some areas may use frequencies not listed here. For complete information on frequencies and usage, consult the *Compendium of American Railroad Frequencies* by Gary Sturm and Mark Landgraf, available at local hobby shops or by mail from a variety of vendors *(see Appendix G)*.

Railroads marked with an asterisk are currently undergoing merger or corporate restructuring. Therefore, frequencies and operations are subject to change.

ABERDEEN, CAROLINA & WESTERN	160.680; 461.450; 466.450
ALASKA RAILROAD	161.335; 165.265; 165.335; 164.625
ALGOMA CENTRAL	160.530; 160.575; 160.605
ALLEGHENY & EASTERN	160.290; 160.425
AMTRAK	160.920 or HOST RR FREQS
APALACHICOLA NORTHERN	160.380; 160.500
ARIZONA & CALIFORNIA	160.860
ARIZONA EASTERN	160.215; 160.275; 160.530
ARKANSAS & MISSOURI	160.440; 160.785; 161.475
AUSTIN & NORTHWESTERN	160.305; 161.520
BC TRANSIT	410.2875; 415.0625; 416.0625
BANGOR & AROOSTOOK	160.440; 160.740; 160.920
BAY COLONY	160.800; 161.265; 161.305
BESSEMER & LAKE ERIE	160.830; 161.310
BOSTON & MAINE*	161.160; 161.400; 161.520
BRITISH COLUMBIA	159.570; 160.695; 161.235; 161.520

BUFFALO & PITTSBURGH	160.230; 160.320; 160.530
BURLINGTON NORTHERN*	160.695; 161.100; 161.160; 161.250
CALIFORNIA NORTHERN	160.635; 161.385
CALTRANS	161.550
CANADIAN AMERICAN	160.425; 161.115; 161.475; 161.535
CANADIAN NATIONAL	160.545; 160.935; 161.205; 161.415
CANADIAN PACIFIC	160.425; 161.115; 161.325; 161.475
CAPE BRETON & CENTRAL N.S.	160.050; 160.980; 161.310
CARTIER	160.800; 161.130
CEDAR VALLEY RAILROAD*	160.605; 161.535
CENTRAL WESTERN	160.590; 161.445
CHICAGO & ILLINOIS MIDLAND	160.290; 160.950
CHICAGO & NORTHWESTERN*	160.455; 160.890; 161.040
CHICAGO CENTRAL*	160.755; 161.190
COLUMBUS & GREENVILLE	160.230; 160.245
CONRAIL	160.800; 160.980; 161.070
CSX	160.230; 160.290; 160.320; 161.370
D&I	161.190
DAKOTA, MINNESOTA & EASTERN	160.395; 160.965
DAKOTA, MO. VALLEY & WESTERN	160.305; 161.265
DAKOTA SOUTHERN	161.535
DELAWARE & HUDSON*	160.530; 160.590; 161.100; 161.475
DULUTH, MISSABE & IRON RANGE.	160.230; 160.350; 160.800
DULUTH, WINNIPEG & PACIFIC*	161.205; 161.415; 161.550
ELGIN, JOLIET & EASTERN	160.260; 160.350
ESCANABA & LAKE SUPERIOR	160.320
EUREKA SOUTHERN	160.775; 161.520; 161.550
FERROCARRILES NAC. MEXICO	167.100; 173.225; 173.325
FINGER LAKES	161.100
FLORIDA EAST COAST	160.530; 160.650
GO TRANSIT	413.9375 OR HOST RR FREQS
GATEWAY WESTERN	160.725; 161.280; 161.295; 161.460
GEORGIA CENTRAL	160.680; 160.800
GEORGIA NORTHEASTERN	461.250; 466.250
GEORGIA SOUTHWESTERN	160.335, 161.085, 161.325
GRAINBELT	161.100; 161.520
GRAND TRUNK WESTERN*	160.530; 160.590; 160.845
GREATER WINNIPEG	167.670; 167.700
HOUSATONIC	160.395, 161.505

HURON & EASTERN	160.440
ILLINOIS CENTRAL*	160.920; 161.190; 161.460
INDIANA & OHIO	160.575; 161.385
INDIANA HI-RAIL*	160.590; 160.695; 160.845
INDIANA	161.100
IOWA INTERSTATE	160.230; 160.305; 161.220; 161.610
IOWA NORTHERN	161.610
IOWA	161.220
KANKAKEE, BEAVERVILLE & SOU	160.215
KANSAS CITY SOUTHERN	160.215; 160.545; 160.590; 161.085
KANSAS SOUTHWESTERN	160.995
KIAMICHI*	160.920
KYLE	160.275; 160.320; 160.935
LAKES STATES	161.310
LONG ISLAND	160.380; 161.265; 161.445
MAINE CENTRAL*	160.380; 160.620; 161.250
MARTA	160.230; 160.320
MARYLAND & DELAWARE	160.695
MBTA	161.310
MC CLOUD RIVER	160.025; 160.680
METRA	160.770; 161.040; 161.100; 161.520
METRO-NORTH	160.410; 160.950; 161.220; 161.280
MINNESOTA CENTRAL	160.305; 161.265
MO. & NORTHERN ARKANSAS	160.245; 160.635; 160.980
MOHAWK, ADIRONDACK & NO.	160.470; 160.920; 161.280; 161.460
MONTANA RAIL LINK	160.950, 161.160, 161.340
NASHVILLE & EASTERN	160.365; 160.560
NEW ENGLAND CENTRAL	160.935; 161.040; 161.205; 161.415
NEW JERSEY TRANSIT	160.440; 160.800; 160.830; 161.400
NORFOLK SOUTHERN	160.245; 160.440; 161.190; 161.250
NORTHEAST KANSAS & MO.	160.815
OHIO CENTRAL	160.845
ONTARIO NORTHLAND	160.545; 160.995; 161.265
PADUCAH & LOUISVILLE	160.740
PITTSBURG & SHAWMUT	160.740; 161.160
PROVIDENCE & WORCESTER	160.650; 161.100
QUE., NORTH SHORE & LABR.	159.810; 160.215; 160.290; 160.335
READING & NORTHERN	160.980; 161.310
RED RIVER VALLEY & WESTERN	160.365; 161.295
ROCHESTER & SOUTHERN	160.770; 161.100; 161.445

STCUM (MONTREAL)	169.440; 169.905 OR HOST FREQ
ST. LAWRENCE & ATLANTIC	160.815; 160.965
SAN DIEGO & IMPERIAL VALLEY	160.455
SANTA FE*	160.650; 160.935; 161.190; 161.370
SEPTA	160.350; 160.395; 160.800; 161.460
SOO LINE*	160.770; 161.085; 161.370; 161.520
SOUTH KANSAS & OKLAHOMA	160.785
SOUTHEAST KANSAS	160.785
SOUTHERN OF B.C.	160.275; 160.515; 160.545; 160.605
SOUTHERN PACIFIC*	160.320; 160.920; 161.100; 161.550
SUSQUEHANNA	160.295; 160.485; 160.620; 161.295
TENNESSEE SOUTHERN	160.755
TEXAS & NEW MEXICO	161.520
TEXAS MEXICAN	160.695; 161.220
TEXAS NORTHEASTERN	160.815
TOLEDO, PEORIA & WESTERN	161.310; 161.400
TORONTO TRANSIT	412.0375; 412.0625; 412.1125
TUSCOLA & SAGINAW BAY	160.575; 161.100
UNION PACIFIC*	160.410; 160.470; 160.515; 160.740
UTAH	160.560; 161.145
VIA RAIL	418.050; 451.850; 456.863
VERMONT	160.290; 160.440; 160.710; 161.010
WASHINGTON CENTRAL*	160.770; 161.295
WHEELING & LAKE ERIE	161.025; 161.520
WICHITA, TILLMAN & JACKSON	160.275; 161.265
WISCONSIN & SOUTHERN	160.215; 160.575; 161.145
WISCONSIN CENTRAL	160.260; 160.785; 161.295
WYOMING COLORADO	160.380
YADKIN VALLEY	160.980

APPENDIX B

AAR Channel Designators

The following is a listing of the Association of American Railroads (AAR) channel designators used by U.S. and Canadian railroads. Channels 02 thru 06 are used in Canada only. Listeners located south of the border may experience interference from trucking companies on these channels. Note that all U.S. channels are spaced 0.015 MHz (15 kHz) apart.

Some railroads do not operate on standard AAR channels. These include many industrial, commuter, and government-owned lines.

When programming these frequencies into a scanner, it is usually not necessary to enter the trailing zeroes.

02	159.810	37	160.665	72	161.190
03	159.930	38	160.680	73	161.205
04	160.050	39	160.695	74	161.220
05	160.185	40	160.710	75	161.235
06	160.200	41	160.725	76	161.250
07	160.215	42	160.740	77	161.265
08	160.230	43	160.755	78	161.280
09	160.245	44	160.770	79	161.295
10	160.260	45	160.785	80	161.310
11	160.275	46	160.800	81	161.325
12	160.290	47	160.815	82	161.340
13	160.305	48	160.830	83	161.355
14	160.320	49	160.845	84	161.370
15	160.335	50	160.860	85	161.385
16	160.350	51	160.875	86	161.400
17	160.365	52	160.890	87	161.415
18	160.380	53	160.905	88	161.430
19	160.395	54	160.920	89	161.445
20	160.410	55	160.935	90	161.460
21	160.425	56	160.950	91	161.475
22	160.440	57	160.965	92	161.490
23	160.455	58	160.980	93	161.505
24	160.470	59	160.995	94	161.520
25	160.485	60	161.010	95	161.535
26	160.500	61	161.025	96	161.550
27	160.515	62	161.040	97	161.565
28	160.530	63	161.055		
29	160.545	64	161.070		
30	160.560	65	161.085		
31	160.575	66	161.100		
32	160.590	67	161.115		
33	160.605	68	161.130		
34	160.620	69	161.145		
35	160.635	70	161.160		
36	160.650	71	161.175		

APPENDIX C

Coded Squelch Tone Frequencies

Coded squelch tones are identified by industry-standard, alphanumeric codes. Each tone is transmitted continuously at a constant, sub-audible frequency.

FREQUENCY (Hz)	ALPHANUMERIC	NUMERIC
67.0	XZ	01
69.3	WZ	NONE
71.9	XA	02
74.4	WA	03
77.0	XB	04
79.7	WB	05
82.5	YZ	06
85.4	YA	07
88.5	YB	08
91.5	ZZ	09
94.8	ZA	10
97.4	ZB	NONE
100.0	1Z	11
103.5	1A	12
107.2	1B	13
110.9	2Z	14
114.8	2A	15
118.8	2B	16
123.0	3Z	17
127.3	3A	18
131.8	3B	19
136.5	4Z	20
141.3	4A	21
146.2	4B	22
151.4	5Z	23

156.7	5A	24
162.2	5B	25
167.9	6Z	26
173.8	6A	27
179.9	6B	28
186.2	7Z	29
192.8	7A	30
203.5	M1	31
206.5	8Z	NONE
210.7	M2	32
218.1	M3	33
225.7	M4	34
229.1	9Z	NONE
233.6	M5	35
241.8	M6	36
250.3	M7	37
254.1	OZ	NONE

APPENDIX D

Reporting Marks for Selected Railroads

Reporting marks are used in conjunction with equipment numbers to identify a particular car or trailer and its owner or lease holder.

The following is a list of reporting marks for selected railroads. Marks ending with "X" represent cars owned by private (non-rail operating) companies. "Z" endings (not listed here) represent intermodal trailers, e.g. CSXZ is a trailer owned or leased by CSX Transportation.

ABOX	RAILBOX
ACFX	ACF INDUSTRIES
ACL	ATLANTIC COAST LINE
ADMX	ARCHER-DANIELS-MIDLAND
AEX	ANDERSONS
AMAX	AMAX COAL
AMTK	AMTRAK
AOCX	ALCOA
ATSF	ATCHISON, TOPEKA & SANTA FE
AVL	AROOSTOOK VALLEY
BAR	BANGOR & AROOSTOOK
BCOL	BRITISH COLUMBIA RAIL
BM	BOSTON & MAINE
BN	BURLINGTON NORTHERN
BNFE	WESTERN FRUIT EXPRESS
B&O	BALTIMORE & OHIO
CAGX	CON-AGRA
CAGY	COLUMBUS & GREENVILLE
CC	CHICAGO CENTRAL
CGW	CHICAGO GREAT WESTERN
CHTT	CHICAGO HEIGHTS TERMINAL TRANSFER

CN	CANADIAN NATIONAL
CNIS	CANADIAN NATIONAL INTL. SERVICE
CNLX	CANADIAN NATIONAL LEASING
CNW	CHICAGO NORTHWESTERN
CNWX	CANADIAN NATIONAL WHEAT
C&O	CHESAPEAKE & OHIO
CP	CANADIAN PACIFIC
CR	CONRAIL
CS	COLORADO SOUTHERN
CRDX	CHICAGO FREIGHTCAR LEASING
CRGX	CARGILL
CRLE	COE RAIL
CV	CENTRAL VERMONT
D&H	DELAWARE & HUDSON
DODX	U.S. DEPARTMENT OF DEFENSE
DOWX	DOW CHEMICAL
DRGW	DENVER & RIO GRANDE WESTERN
DTI	DETROIT, TOLEDO & IRONTON
DUPX	DUPONT
DWC	DULUTH, WINNIPEG & PACIFIC
EL	ERIE LACKAWANNA
ELS	ESCANABA & LAKE SUPERIOR
FEC	FLORIDA EAST COAST
FGER	FRUIT GROWERS EXPRESS
FGMR	FRUIT GROWERS MECHANICAL REFRIGERATOR
GATX	GENERAL AMERICAN TRANSPORTATION
GCTX	GENERAL CHEMICAL
GONX	RAILGON
GTW	GRAND TRUNK WESTERN
GVSR	GALVESTON
GWIX	GENESEE & WYOMING INDUSTRIES
HATX	HELM LEASING
HLMX	HELM LEASING
IC	ILLINOIS CENTRAL
ICG	ILLINOIS CENTRAL GULF
IMCX	INTERNATIONAL MINERALS
KCS	KANSAS CITY SOUTHERN
LVRC	LAMOILLE VALLEY
MDTX	MERCHANTS DESPATCH TRANSPORTATION
MEC	MAINE CENTRAL

MILW	MILWAUKEE ROAD
MKT	MISSOURI-KANSAS-TEXAS
MOBX	MOBIL OIL
MP	MISSOURI PACIFIC
MRL	MONTANA RAIL LINK
MSDR	MISSISSIPPI DELTA
MSRC	MID-SOUTH RAIL
NATX	NORTH AMERICAN TRANSPORTATION
NOKL	NORTHWESTERN OKLAHOMA
NP	NORTHERN PACIFIC
NS	NORFOLK SOUTHERN
N&W	NORFOLK & WESTERN
NYSW	SUSQUEHANNA
PAL	PADUCAH & LOUISVILLE
PFE	PACIFIC FRUIT EXPRESS
PLCX	GENERAL ELECTRIC RAILCAR
PPGX	PPG INDUSTRIES
PROX	PROCOR LTD.
PRR	PENNSYLVANIA
QC	QUEBEC CENTRAL
RBOX	RAILBOX
RDG	READING
RPCX	RALSTON PURINA
RUSX	USL CAPITAL RAILCAR
SAL	SEABOARD AIR LINE
SCL	SEABOARD COAST LINE
SBD	SEABOARD SYSTEM
SIRX	SOUTHERN ILLINOIS RAILCAR
SLR	ST. LAWRENCE & ATLANTIC
SLSF	FRISCO
SM	SAINT MARYS
SOO	SOO LINE
SOU	SOUTHERN
SP	SOUTHERN PACIFIC
SPFE	SOUTHERN PACIFIC FRUIT EXPRESS
SSAM	SAULT STE. MARIE
SSW	COTTON BELT
STMX	A.E. STALEY
TASD	ALABAMA STATE DOCKS

TOE	TEXAS OKLAHOMA & EASTERN
TSBY	TUSCOLA & SAGINAW BAY
TSRD	TWIN STATE
TTX	TRAILER TRAIN
UP	UNION PACIFIC
UPFE	UNION PACIFIC FRUIT EXPRESS
USLX	GENERAL ELECTRIC RAILCAR
UTLX	UNION TANK CAR
VCY	VENTURA COUNTY
WC	WISCONSIN CENTRAL
WCTR	WHITE CITY TERMINAL & UTILITY
WE	WHEELING & LAKE ERIE
WLO	WATERLOO
WM	WESTERN MARYLAND
WP	WESTERN PACIFIC

APPENDIX E

Sample Train Symbols

The following is the itinerary for CR 889280, a Conrail grain hopper, as it traveled the rail system between March and June of 1994. Note how train symbols denote either train type or origination and destination.

DATE	LOCATION	STATUS	TRAIN	NOTES
3-12	S. BYRON, NY	EMPTY	------	PLACED AT PATRON
3-15	ROCHESTER, NY	LOADED	WARO-16	ARRIVING
3-18	ROCHESTER, NY	LOADED	SEBU-7	DEPARTING
3-18	BUFFALO, NY	LOADED	SEBU-7	ARRIVING
3-20	BUFFALO, NY	LOADED	BUPI-1X	LEAVING
3-21	ASHTABULA, OH	LOADED	BUPI-1X	LEAVING
3-21	CONWAY, PA	LOADED	BUPI-1X	ARRIVING
3-23	CONEMAUGH, PA	LOADED	PIBA-3	ARRIVING
3-23	ENOLA, PA	LOADED	PIBA-3	ARRIVING
3-25	DILLERVILLE, PA	LOADED	WHLA-46	ARRIVING
3-26	LANCASTER, PA	LOADED	------	CNSTRCTVLY PLACED
3-30	LANCASTER, PA	LOADED	------	PLACED AT PATRON
4-18	LANCASTER, PA	LOADED	------	RELEASD FM PATRON
4-29	E. CONWAY, PA	LOADED	XXEAST	ARRIVING
5-1	HARRISBURG, PA	LOADED	PIMO	ARRIVING
5-2	HARRISBURG, PA	LOADED	YHHB-79	DEPARTING
5-3	ROCKVILLE, PA	LOADED	YHHB-79	ARRIVING
5-4	NRTHMBRLND, PA	LOADED	BUHB-3	DEPARTING
5-5	NRTHMBRLND, PA	LOADED	------	INTRCHNGD TO NSHR
5-24	NRTHMBRLND, PA	LOADED	------	INTRCHNGD FM NSHR
5-26	NRTHMBRLND, PA	EMPTY	BUHB-5	DEPARTING
5-26	ROCKVILLE, PA	EMPTY	HBPI-6X	DEPARTING
5-27	CONWAY, PA	EMPTY	HBPI-6X	ARRIVING
5-28	CONWAY, PA	EMPTY	PIEL-8X	DEPARTING

5-28	ELKHART, IN	EMPTY	PIEL-8X	ARRIVING	
5-30	TLDO-STNLY, OH	EMPTY	ELTO	ARRIVING	
5-31	TLDO-AIRLNE, OH	EMPTY	YDAL-11	ARRIVING	
6-1	TOLEDO, OH	LOADED	------	RLSD FROM PATRON	
6-9	TLDO-STNLEY, OH	LOADED	YDAL-11	ARRIVING	
6-12	TLDO DOCK, OH	LOADED	------	INTRCHNGD TO CSXT	

KEY:

BUHB-3	BUFFALO–HARRISBURG, ORIGINATED MAY 3
BUPI-1X	BUFFALO–PITTSBURGH, ORIGINATED MAR 1, EXTRA SECTION 1
CSXT	CSX TRANSPORTATION
ELTO	ELKHART–TOLEDO
HBPI-6X	HARRISBURG–PITTSBURGH, ORIG'D MAY 6, EXTRA SECTION 1
NSHR	NORTH SHORE RAILROAD
PIBA-3	PITTSBURGH–BALTIMORE, ORIGINATED MAR 3
PIEL-8X	PITTSBURGH–ELKHART, ORIG'D MAY 8, EXTRA SECTION 1
PIMO	PITTSBURGH–MORRISVILLE, PA.
SEBU-7	SELKIRK, NY–BUFFALO, ORIGINATED MAR 7
WARO-16	WAYFREIGHT, ALBANY DIVISION, ROCHESTER ASSIGNMENT 16
WHLA-46	WAYFREIGHT, HARRISBURG DIV., LANCASTER ASSIGNMENT 46
XXEAST	EMPTY TRAIN X, EASTBOUND
YDAL-11	YARD TRAIN, DEARBORN DIV., AIR LINE YARD ASSIGNMENT 11
YHHB-79	YARD TRAIN, HARRISBURG DIV., HARRISBURG YARD ASSGN 79

APPENDIX F

Rules Governing Radio Use

Radio use on railroads is governed by both Federal and company regulations, as represented in the following paragraphs. This information is not official and therefore *must not be used* by any employees in the discharge of their duties.

Radio General and Operating Rules (Federal)

Association of American Railroads,
Operations and Maintenance Department,
Operating-Transportation Division,
Communication and Signal Section

Adopted by the Federal Communications Commission on August 21, 1945, and attached to its Order No. 126 pertaining to operation of railroad radio equipment by railroad employees in connection with railroad operations.

General

The following rules and requirements cover use of railroad radio systems and govern employees using such systems:

A. Definition: A Railroad Radio Communication system is one employing radio for the transmission of intelligence between moving equipment, between moving equipment and a fixed point, or between fixed points.

B. Radio communication systems are under the jurisdiction of the Federal Communications Commission. The railroad company and its employees are governed by the Commission's Operating Rules. Violation is a Federal offense for which severe penalties are provided.

Operating Rules

1. All employees, except those specifically authorized to do so, are prohibited from making any adjustments to a railroad radio set. Employees

so authorized must carry their FCC operator license or verification card when on duty. If it appears that a radio transmitter is not operating properly its use shall be discontinued and the designated railroad official notified as soon as possible.

2. No employee shall knowingly transmit any false distress communication, any unnecessary, irrelevant or unidentified communication, nor utter any obscene, indecent, or profane language via radio.

3. No employee shall divulge or publish the existence, contents, purport, effect or meaning of any communication (distress communications excluded) except to the person for whom the communication is intended or to another employee of the railroad whose duties may require knowledge of the communication. The above applies either to communications received direct or to any that may be intercepted.

4. Before transmitting any employee operating a radio transmitting set shall listen a sufficient interval to be sure that the circuit is not already in use, particularly for distress traffic.

5. A distress call will be preceded by the word "Emergency" repeated three times. Such calls shall be used only to cover initial reports of derailments, storms, washouts, fires, obstructions to tracks, or other matters which would cause serious delay to traffic, damage to property, injury to employees or the travelling public, and shall contain as complete information thereon as possible. All employees shall give absolute priority to communications from another station in distress, and except in answering or aiding a station in distress shall refrain from sending any communication until there is assurance that no interference will result to the station in distress.

6. The Railroad Company is required to answer an official notice of violation of the terms of the Communications Act of 1934, as amended, within ten days from receipt of notice and any violation shall answer such inquiry within 24 hours after receipt of notice.

7. Any employee shall permit inspection of the radio equipment in his charge and all FCC documents pertaining thereto, by a duly accredited representative of the Federal Communications Commission at any reasonable time.

8. Employees, except in yard operation, shall identify the radio station from which they are calling by prefacing their call with the railroad name, for example, "ABC (Railroad) Caboose Train 92 calling Engine," "XYZ (Railroad Caboose Train 92 calling Engine Train 89," or "MAIN (Railroad) Engine 547 calling Caboose 1402."

9. In certain cases at crossings, junctions or paralleling tracks some interference may develop with another railroad. In such cases especial care in making identification shall be used and the employees concerned shall cooperate in handling their business by alternating calls and being brief as possible.

10. If any communication from a station other than another railroad radio station interferes with Railroad Radio service the railroad employee will endeavor to ascertain the identity of such station and report the occurrence as soon as possible through authorized channels, to the designated railroad official, giving the exact time, nature of the communication and identity of the station, if possible.

Internationally, the word "MAYDAY" indicates a distress message, the word "PAN," an urgent message and the word "SECURITY," a safety message. Railroad employees hearing such messages must report them immediately through authorized channels to the designated railroad official in addition to taking such appropriate action to relieve the distress as may be possible.

NORAC Operating Rules (Company)

Northeast Operating Rules Advisory Committee

Protection of Trains

136. Emergency Stops: Protection

a. Radio Transmission

When a train is moving and emergency application of the brakes occurs, crew members must immediately protect adjacent tracks by initiating an emergency radio transmission, in the manner of the following example:

"Emergency, Emergency, Emergency. Train TV-24 engine 6605 is in emergency moving east on No. 2 track at MP 78."

Movement Permit Form D

The Dispatcher issues Form D's to restrict or authorize movements. Form D's are also issued to convey instructions in situations not covered in the Operating Rules.

165. Form D Delivery

The dispatcher may personally deliver Form D to addressed employees, or he may transmit Form D to an Operator, who will then be responsible for delivering the Form D. Form D may be physically delivered to addressed employees; it may be dictated to them by radio, telephone, or in person; or it may be delivered to them by electronic transmission.

b. Dictation of Form D by Radio, Telephone, or in Person

Form D's may be dictated only to employees who are qualified on the Operating Rules. Form D's must not be dictated to or copied by an employee operating the controls of a moving train.

When dictating and repeating Form D's, employees must read aloud and plainly pronounce all applicable preprinted and written portions. Numerals in lines 1 through 13 of Form D's must be pronounced digit by digit. For example, "105" will be pronounced "one-zero-five."

Before dictating a Form D, the Dispatcher must specify the number of copies to be made if more than one copy is required. The Dispatcher must not give "Time Effective" until the Form D has been repeated correctly. Once the Dispatcher has given his name, receiving employees must repeat immediately from their copy in the same order they were addressed, unless otherwise directed.

Employees must listen while other addressees repeat Form D and call attention to any discrepancies. Once all addressees have repeated Form D correctly, the Dispatcher will give "Time Effective," which must then be repeated by the receiving employees.

When a Form D is dictated to an employee on a train, the receiving employee must ensure that employees on the train who are addressed in the Form D receive a copy of it before reaching the first location where employees must act upon the Form D. If physical delivery of the Form D is not practical, the receiving employee must dictate the Form D information to other employees addressed, who must copy and repeat the Form D information.

When Form D's are relayed by employees, the dictating employee must follow the procedures outlined above for Dispatchers. "Time Effective" must not be transmitted until the receiving employee correctly repeats the Form D.

Radios and Telephones

Radio use must comply with regulations of the Federal Communications Commission (FCC). The following rules are set forth to meet these regulations and to protect a safe and efficient operation.

700. Radio Use

Company radios must be used exclusively for railroad operations. The use of radios other than those furnished by the Company for railroad operations is prohibited.

701. Radio Failure and Interference

If the radio fails, other means of communication must be used to avoid delay in operations. Failure of radio or interference from another radio station must be reported to the Dispatcher or Yardmaster promptly with information as to location, time, and, if possible, the identity of the interfering station.

702. Care and Protection of Radio Equipment

Employees using radio equipment must exercise care to prevent damage to or loss of the equipment. Employees assigned a portable radio will be responsible for the proper care and protection of it.

703. Technical Adjustment of Radios

No technical adjustments may be made to a radio set, except by those employees specifically authorized.

704. Radio Inspection

Employees shall permit inspection of the radio equipment in their charge and all FCC documents pertaining thereto by a duly accredited representative of the FCC at any reasonable time.

705. Radio Transmission and Reception Procedures

When taking charge of a radio, employees must make a voice test with another radio unit to confirm quality and readability of transmissions. If the radio does not operate properly, it must be removed from service until repaired, and each crew member and Dispatcher or Yardmaster notified promptly. In event of radio failure en route, the Dispatcher must be notified as soon as practical.

Before transmitting by radio, the employee must listen to ensure that the channel on which he intends to transmit is not in use.

All transmissions must be repeated by the employee receiving them except:

1. Transmissions used in yard and switching operations.

2. Those transmissions that do not contain any information, instruction or advice that could affect the safety of a railroad operation.

Employees must ensure that radio contact with the proper persons has been made and must not take action until certain that all conversation with them has been heard, understood and acknowledged.

Any radio communication that is not fully understood or completed in accordance with the requirements of these rules shall not be acted upon and shall be treated as though not sent. Emergency communications are an exception.

706. Radio Location and Monitoring

When their duties involve the use of radio, employees must have the radio on and tuned to the proper channel at all times. The volume must be adjusted so that all transmissions can be heard.

The Timetable designates fixed base stations, wayside stations, periods attended and assigned radio channels.

All employees shall give absolute priority to emergency communications. Except in answering or aiding a station in distress, employees shall refrain from sending any communication until certain that no interference will result to the station in distress.

708. Radio Messages: Content and Code Words

The following procedures will govern identification and content of messages when using radio:

To originate a call, employees must:

1. Identify their employing railroad

2. Identify their base station, wayside station or yard station by name or other designation of station and location.

3. Identify their mobile radio unit by:

a. Schedule number if on a scheduled train.
b. Symbol and engine number if on an extra train.
c. TC followed by the number of the car if on a track car.
d. Other appropriate mobile unit identification.

Communication must be as brief as possible and must use these key words:

"ROGER"   to signify that the message was received and understood. When required by Rule 705, "ROGER" also means that you have repeated instructions correctly.

"OVER"   at the close of each transmission to which a response is expected.

"OUT"   at the close of each transmission to which a response is not necessary. "OUT" must be preceded by proper identification.

"EMERGENCY"   transmitted three times to obtain use of radio channels for initial report of conditions endangering train movements.

709. Prohibited Transmissions

Employees shall not knowingly transmit:

1. Any false distress communication.

2. Any unnecessary, irrelevant, or unidentified communication.

3. Any obscene, indecent, or profane remark.

710. Radio Communication in the Yard

When positive identification is achieved in connection with switching, classification, and similar operations wholly within a yard, fixed and mobile units may use short identification after the initial transmission and acknowledgement. Short identification must include engine or unit number, such as "Back up 8271" or "Go ahead 8271."

If an exchange of communications continues without substantial interruption, positive identification must be repeated every 15 minutes.

711. Radio Communication in Lieu of Hand Signals

When radio communication is used in lieu of hand signals in connection with the switching, backing or pushing of trains, the employee directing the movement shall give complete instructions or keep in continuous radio contact with the employees receiving the instructions. If the instructions are not understood or continuous radio contact is not maintained, the movement must be stopped immediately and may not be resumed until the misunderstanding has been resolved or communication has been restored. If the means of communication is changed, no movement may be made until all crew members have been notified.

When backing or pushing a train, the distance of the movement must be specified, and the movement must stop in one-half the specified distance unless additional instructions are received.

Names of fixed signals affecting the movement of a train must be communicated to the Engineer.

712. Signal Indications

Dispatchers or Operators must not advise the aspect, name, or indication of any fixed signal, and crew members must not request this information. Crew members may use the radio to communicate a fixed signal to other members of the same crew.

Radio communication may not be used to convey instructions that would have the effect of overriding the indication of a fixed signal. Radio communication may only be used to impose a more restrictive action than the indication of a fixed signal.

713. Radio Communication Concerning Passing Trains

A Dispatcher or Operator may accept information regarding the movement of a train from:

1. The Conductor or Engineer of another train or

2. A Track Car Driver or

3. Another qualified employee.

When necessary to report the passage of a train prior to fouling or occupying a track, employees must identify the passing train by engine number and proper marker display. Dispatchers or Operators must not give permission for a train to foul or occupy a track until this information is received.

Appendix G

Information Sources

Magazines covering national railroad news, operations, railroad related products, including books:

Extra 2200 South
P.O. Box 1004
Garibaldi Highlands, B.C. V0N 1T0

The Railroad Press
1150 Carlisle Street, #444
Hanover, Penna. 17331

The Shortline
P.O. Box 607
Pleasant Garden, N.C. 27313

Railfan & Railroad
P.O. Box 700
Newton, N.J. 07860

Rail Classics
P.O. Box 16149
North Hollywood, Calif. 91606

Trains
P.O. Box 1612
Waukesha, Wisc. 53187

Railway Age
1809 Capitol Avenue
Omaha, Nebr. 68102

Magazines covering radio communications, monitoring, scanners, antennas, accessories, and related products, including books:

Popular Communications
76 North Broadway
Hicksville, N.Y. 11801

Monitoring Times
Grove Enterprises, Inc.
P.O. Box 98
Brasstown, N.C. 28902

Radio
700 One Tandy Center
Fort Worth, Tex. 76102

Amateur Radio Trader
P.O. Box 3729
Crossville, Tenn. 38557

Appendix H

Glossary of Terms

Railroaders, like those in most large professions, have developed a colorful language of their own. This jargon is used in everyday conversations, including radio messages.

absolute block—a block that must not be occupied by more than one train at a time (see block)

air hose—hose used to transfer train line air from car to car (see train line; gladhands)

Alco—a locomotive manufactured by Alco Products or Montreal Locomotive Works

alertor—pushbutton or similar device that must be periodically actuated by a locomotive engineer to avoid a shutdown of the locomotive; used to prevent accidents caused by dozing or sleeping crews; also called deadman

alley—a clear track in a yard

amputate—to uncouple cars or locomotives from a train

anchor—to set the handbrakes on a car

annul—to cancel a train

armstrong—any manually operated mechanical device

aspects—signal appearance that conveys an indication (see indication)

assistant engineer—formerly called a locomotive fireman, now used only on long-haul passenger trains

automatic block signal (ABS)—a signal that is activated either by track circuits or in conjunction with interlocking or controlled point circuits; this block signal automatically indicates track condition and block occupancy (see track circuit; controlled point; interlocking; block)

automatic train stop (ATS)–a device on a locomotive that automatically applies the train brakes when an engineer fails to acknowledge a restrictive signal

B&B–department responsible for maintaining buildings and bridges

bad order–defective equipment; to withdraw defective equipment from service; also called a cripple

baggage-dormitory–a passenger car that contains storage space for baggage and sleeping quarters for the crew

ballast–any material, usually cinders or stones, used to support, cushion, and stabilize track structures

ballast cleaner–a track-mounted vehicle used by MOW to clean and recycle ballast (see maintenance-of-way)

ballast regulator–a track-mounted vehicle used by MOW to replace and redistribute ballast; also called a regulator (see maintenance-of-way)

balloon track–a loop of track used to reverse the direction of a train (see wye)

beanery–an eatery frequented by rail personnel

beans–a lunch or dinner break

bend iron–to throw a track switch (see switch)

big hole–an emergency brake application; also called wipe the clock, dump the air (see emergency braking)

big hook–company wrecking crane

binders–handbrakes (see anchor)

black diamonds–coal

black hole–railroad tunnel

blazer–blazing journal box (see journal box; hot box)

bleed–to drain the air from an air tank

blinker–illuminated marker (see marker)

block–a length of track with defined limits on which train movements are governed by block signals, cab signals, or Form D; a cut of classified cars (see absolute block; cab signal; Form D; cut; classification)

block signal–a fixed signal displayed to trains at the entrance of a block to govern the use of the block (see aspect; indication; fixed signal; block)

blue flag–a blue flag, tag, or light displayed on equipment to indicate the presence of workers on, under, or between equipment

bolted rail–see jointed rail

bombs–locomotives and railcars manufactured by Bombardier

bond–any electrical connection made to a rail or, on jointed rail, between rails (see jointed rail)

booster–a cabless locomotive used in MU with regular locomotives (see MU)

bowl–the area in a yard beyond the hump where cars are assembled into blocks (see hump; block; classification)

brake line–see train line

branch–short for branchline, a line diverging from a main to serve smaller towns with low traffic density; typically operated at low speeds and with minimal maintenance (see spur; streak of rust)

break up–a radio transmission experiencing weakness, garbling, or interference

brick–handheld portable radio, especially an older model

buff–railroad enthusiast (see foamer)

buggy–caboose; also called hack, van, cabin

bull–railroad police detective; also called dick, cinder dick

bulletin order–a publication used to notify employees of changes to rules, procedures, or other instructions affecting the movement of trains

bunching the slack–an action by a locomotive engineer wherein the space between cars, or slack, is minimized by compressing the drawbars to facilitate starting a train on grades (see drawbar; stretching the slack)

bungalow–any small, trackside structure housing control, signalling, or communications equipment; also called a wayside shack

C&E–conductor and engineer; **C&S**–communication & signal dept.

COFC–container-on-flatcar freight, whereby an intermodal (i.e., ship-rail-truck) shipping container is placed directly on a flatcar (see TOFC; piggyback)

CTC–centralized traffic control, a method of controlling and dispatching an entire railroad or sections of a railroad from a single control center

cab–short for locomotive cab or taxicab

cab signal–a signal located in a locomotive cab that indicates track occupancy or condition; cab signals are used in conjunction with interlocking signals or in lieu of block signals (see interlocking; block signal)

cab unit–locomotive with a full-width hood used almost exclusively in passenger operations; the walkway is located inside the locomotive (see walkway; hood unit)

cabin–caboose; also called buggy, hack, van

caboose hop–a train consisting only of an engine and a caboose

caller–person responsible for calling personnel to assemble a train crew; also called crew caller

camp car–any on-track vehicle, except a work train, used to house railroad employees, usually MOW personnel (see MOW)

Canadian cab–a locomotive cab with a full-width nose and a standard control stand (see control stand; safety cab)

car knocker–car inspector

car length–a measurement for estimating the space between cars, equal to approximately 50 feet; used for relating distance to a backing locomotive; typically heard in brakeman-engineer radio communications; zero car lengths is known as on the pin

car numbers–identification numbers assigned to every car in interline service; painted or stencilled on the sides and ends of all rail cars along with car reporting marks (see reporting marks)

catenary–overhead electrical lines and associated hardware that supply power to electric locomotives, especially those parts that contact the pantograph (see pantograph)

catwalk–walkway on top of covered hoppers and older boxcars (see hopper)

Century–a line of diesel locomotives manufactured by Alco Products

class lights–multicolor lights mounted on locomotives, usually at both ends, to indicate the class or status of a train

classification–the process of organizing and assembling cars into blocks according to destination; blocks are then combined to form a train (see block)

clearance–permission to occupy a section of track with a train or track car; the maximum permissible height and width of railcars or lading on a particular stretch of track (see orders)

company varnish–private, company-owned passenger cars for use by railroad executives and customers

conductor–train crewman responsible for the proper operation of a train

consist–collectively, the cars and locomotives that comprise a train

control stand–a pedestal-like device anchored to the floor of a locomotive containing gauges, indicators, and the locomotive's control apparatus (see desktop control; safety cab; Canadian cab)

control station–the dispatcher's office or the location where an operator is on duty from which remote control signal appliances or switches are operated (see tower)

controlled point (CP)–a station designated in the timetable where signals are remote-controlled from a control station (see control station; timetable)

controlled siding (CS)–a circuited siding in which both ends are controlled and governed by signals under the control of a dispatcher or operator (see siding)

controlled signal—a fixed signal that displays a stop signal as selected by a dispatcher or operator (see aspect; indication)

cool your heels—to be placed into a siding or passing track by the dispatcher; also called stabbed, in the hole (see siding; passing track)

counting ties—inspecting a train on foot; also called counting axles (see hit the cinders

couple—to join locomotives and cars to form a train; also called couple up

coupler—the device at the end of a drawbar that physically joins railroad cars and locomotives (see drawbar; knuckle draft gear)

crew change—the action whereby one crew replaces or relieves another; the place where this occurs

crew kit—a small kit, usually packed in a plastic bag, containing personal articles for use by train crews including toilet paper, drinking cups, hand towels, etc.

cripple—defective equipment; to withdraw defective equipment from service; also called bad order

crossover—a combination of two switches and associated track interconnecting two adjacent tracks; when lined correctly, the switches and track allow trains to cross from one track to another (see line; turnout)

cut—a string of coupled cars (see block)

DS—abbreviation for train dispatcher (see dispatcher; RTC)

daisy pickers—trespassers, usually on the property to hike, pick flowers, view wildlife, fish, etc. (see trespassers; rockers; vandals)

dark territory—trackage without signalling or a deactivated signal system; movements are usually governed by train orders (see train orders; block signals)

deadline—a section of track used to store retired locomotives and cars

deadman—any protective device, such as a footpedal or pushbutton, that must be continually activated to avoid shutting down locomotives, thus preventing accidents caused by inattention (see alertor)

derailer—a protective device that prevents cars stored in sidings and spurs from fouling other tracks by derailing any car that passes over it; also called a derail (see foul; spur; siding)

desktop control—a desktop-style control console supporting gauges, indicators, and the locomotive's control apparatus (see control stand; safety cab)

detector—a protective device that automatically inspects trains for hot boxes, high-and-wide loads, dragging equipment; also called a dragger (see hot box; high-and-wide; dragging equipment)

diamond—track hardware that allows one track to cross another at grade; also called a frog

dick—railroad police detective; also called bull; cinder dick

dispatcher—short for train dispatcher, the person responsible for directing and routing trains over a defined section of railroad; also called rail traffic controller (RTC)

distant signal—a fixed signal used to govern the approach of a train to a home signal (see block signal)

ditch lights—lights, usually mounted on a locomotive pilot, to increase the area of illumination in front of a locomotive for improved nighttime visibility; also increases the visibility of trains approaching grade crossings (see pilot; grade crossing)

division—that portion of a railroad under the control and supervision of a Superintendent

division point—the dividing line between divisions; usually marked by the presence of offices and other facilities

dogcatchers—crew dispatched to relieve a crew that has exceeded the Federal hours-of-service law (see outlaw; hours-of-service law)

double—to divide a train into sections, which are then moved over the hill individually and reassembled, in order to move the train over a steep grade

double-stack—a method of transporting containers whereby two shipping containers are stacked, one on another, and placed into a well car; also called stacks (see wells; stack train; filet)

draft gear–a cushioning device that facilitates drawbar compression by minimizing mechanical shock when the slack is bunched (see drawbar; bunching the slack; stretching the slack)

drag–a heavy, slow-moving train carrying non-time-sensitive freight (see hotshot)

dragger–see detector

dragging equipment–any objects, such as car wheels, axles, lading, lading restraints, etc., dragging along the ground as a train traverses the tracks

drawbar–the part of rail car that supports a coupler at one end and a connection to draft gear at the other; most cars have a drawbar at each end (see coupler; draft gear; knuckle)

drill–to move a cut of cars into a rail yard

drill crew–a yard switch crew

drop–a switching move in which cars are uncoupled from a locomotive and allowed to coast into place (see switch)

drop off–to leave cars on a siding or at in interchange (see siding; interchange; pickup)

dual control switch–a remote-controlled switch that can also be hand-operated (see switch)

dump the air–to quickly reduce the air pressure in a train line in order to effect an emergency brake application; also called big hole, wipe the clock (see train line; emergency braking)

dwarf–a small, ground-mounted signal typically used in yards and at switches leading into and out of sidings (see mast)

dynamics–short for dynamic breaking, a method of braking trains by dissipating the energy generated by a locomotive's traction motors into an electrical resistance or grid (see independent brake)

dynamiter–a defective car that goes into emergency whenever the brakes are applied; also called a kicker (see emergency braking)

EMD–a locomotive manufactured by the Electro-Motive Division of General Motors Corp.

EOT—abbreviation for end-of-train device, a device mounted on the last car of a train to transmit train line pressure, rear-end motion, and other parameters to an in-cab readout via radio; also contains a marker light; also called a FRED or blinker (see train line; marker)

embargo—an order issued by government agencies or railroads to prohibit the interchange of all or some traffic with a railroad or section of railroad due to strikes, poor track conditions, floods, etc.

emergency braking—a sudden loss of train line pressure, either intentionally or by accident from a broken or disconnected air hose, that causes a full brake application; also called dump the air, big hole, wipe the clock (see air hose; gladhands)

emergency tools—tools for operating remote-controlled switches by hand; usually stored in a trackside tool box (see switch)

empties—empty cars (see loads)

excepted track—track in a an advanced state of deterioration, speeds are usually limited to less than ten mph and freight-only operation

executive train—special passenger train carrying railroad executives and customers; also called office train (see inspection train)

extra—a non-scheduled train or an additional section of a scheduled train

extra board—a roster of railroad employees available for work on an on-call basis

eye—trackside signals, especially those consisting of a single signal that displays multiple aspects (see aspects; indication; block signal)

FRED—abbreviation for flashing rear-end device; also called an EOT, blinker (see EOT)

filet—to remove the top container in a double-stack to satisfy clearance requirements (see double-stack; clearance)

fixed signal—a signal at a fixed location used to control train movements

fireman—see assistant engineer

flag—to hold a red flag or fusee to protect the rear end of a train or a train running through a grade crossing (see fusee)

flagstop—a non-scheduled stop wherein a train stops only in response to a predetermined signal

flat—short for flatcar

flat wheel—a bad order condition in which a non-rotating car wheel has been ground flat by sliding along the railhead (see bad order)

flimsies—train orders, so-called since they are often copied using carbons and onion-skin paper; also called tissues (see train orders)

flying switch—an illegal drop switching move commonly used to move cars to the opposite end of an engine; typically, an engine heads into a siding, couples up, pulls the cars to speed, uncouples, and then quickly accelerates beyond a switch which is immediately thrown to allow the cars to coast onto an adjacent track; after the cars clear the switch, the switch is thrown again, allowing the locomotive to clear the switch; the switch is then thrown a third time to allow the locomotive to enter the adjacent track and couple to the cars; unlikely to be discussed on the radio

foamer—an overzealous railroad enthusiast, especially one who conducts himself in an inconsiderate, unsafe, or irresponsible manner

foreign—any car or locomotive not belonging to a host railroad

Form D—train order that may be given verbally and copied in-person, via radio, telephone, or other electronic means; also called a track warrant

Form 19— train order that need not be signed for by train crews; usually hooped-up to train crews on the fly (see orders)

Form 31—train order that must be picked up and signed for in-person by train crews (see orders)

foul—any train, part of a train, or equipment blocking or encroaching upon a rail line (see derail)

friction bearing—older style axle bearing where the axle is supported by a thin film of lubricating oil between the axle and the load-bearing surface; also called journal bearing (see hot box; journal box)

frog—a ramp used to rerail derailed car wheels; track hardware that allows one track to cross another at grade (see diamond)

funnel—a series of tracks that converge into a single point or geographical location

fusee–railroad term for a highway flare, designed to burn for set intervals such as five minutes, ten minutes, etc.; used for signalling and flagging purposes purposes (see flag)

GE–a locomotive manufactured by General Electric

GM–a locomotive manufactured by General Motors

gangway–the walkway running between two locomotives (see walkway)

gantlet–an overlapping of two or more tracks in a confined space, such as a trestle

goat–any locomotive used in captive service such as switching a repair shop

gon–short for a gondola, a car with an open top and low sides, typically used to transport scrap steel, steel rods, ties, rip-rap, etc.

gantry–an overhead structure spanning the trackage to support signals; also called a signal bridge (see mast; block signals)

geep–short for GP (general purpose), a general term for four-axle, hood-type, roadswitching locomotives manufactured by Electro-Motive or General Motors (see hood unit; roadswitcher)

general order–a publication used to summarize changes to timetables or other instructions (see timetable; orders)

geometry train–a type of inspection train that checks track gauge, track structure, etc. (see inspection train)

ghetto grates–steel mesh or screening placed over locomotive and caboose windows to protect crews from missiles thrown by vandals (see rockers; vandals)

gladhands–the device that couples two air hoses (see air hose)

grab irons–handholds attached to the sides and ends of cars and locomotives

grip–bag carried by train crewmen holding food, drink, radios, crew kits, and other personal items (see crew kit)

grit–sand applied to the railhead to increase traction for locomotives (see sander)

ground relay–a protective device on a locomotive that trips whenever electrical short circuits are detected, especially in traction motors, to avoid damage caused by meltdowns and burning

hack–caboose; also called cabin, buggy, van

hazardous car–any car carrying hazardous materials as specified by the National Transportation Safety Board (see hazmat)

hazmat–short for hazardous materials (see hazardous car)

head in–to move a train or cars into a track

heater–see snow melter

helper–any locomotive or set of locomotives added to the front, middle, or end of train to assist movements over steep grades (see pusher)

hi-rail–see track car

high-and-wide–a load or railcar that exceeds predetermined limits on height and width

highball–permission to enter a main line and achieve track speed (see track speed)

high iron–main line rail

hit the cinders–to alight from a train or locomotive; also called hit the grit or hit the ground

hog law–Federal hours-of-service law (see hours-of-service law)

hogger–locomotive engineer

hole–see passing track

home signal–a fixed signal governing the entrance to an interlocking (see block signal)

hood unit–a locomotive consisting of a short hood forming the "nose," a cab immediately behind the short hood, and a long hood containing the engine and electrical apparatus; walkways are located outside the long hood; the short hood usually houses a toilet for road use (see walkway; roadswitcher; switcher; cab unit)

hoop up–to pass orders to a train on the fly

hopper–rail car with high steel sides and unloading hatches at the bottom; can be closed at the top with loading hatches or wide open; used to transport grain, coal, flour, cement, pellets, powders, etc.

hospital train–a train consisting of locomotives or cars bound for repair, rebuild, or scapping facilities

hostle–to move locomotives around a maintenance facility

hostler–person who moves locomotives around a maintenance facility

hotbox–an overheated axle bearing caused by lack of lubrication in a journal or damaged bearings (see journal box; friction bearing; roller bearing)

hotshot–a time-sensitive freight train; also called a manifest, sprint

hours-of-service law–the Federal law that governs the on-duty time for train crews; currently, crews must be relieved of duty at an authorized crew facility within 12 hours of reporting for duty; also called hog law (see dogcatcher; outlaw; short-time crew)

housetrack–track that leads to an enginehouse

hump–a yard facility where cars are classified by allowing them to coast down an incline into a series of tracks called a bowl; the action of classifying cars using a hump (see classification; bowl; trim)

idler–a dummy car in a train consist that protects adjacent cars or locomotives from overlength loads or hazardous materials

in the clear–a train or car that has cleared a switch or frog so that other trains can safely pass the same point

in the color–a train waiting on the main track for permission to proceed

in the hole– a train waiting in a siding for permission to proceed (see stabbed; siding)

independent brake–the brake control in a locomotive that controls only the locomotives' brakes (see dynamics; train line)

indication–the required action conveyed by the aspect of a signal (see aspect)

industrial track–a track other than a main line, running track, siding, or yard track upon which movements must be made at restricted speed

inspection train–special train assembled to inspect the railroad right-of-way, trackside buildings, or the tracks themselves (see geometry train, executive train)

interchange–the transfer of railcars from one railroad to the next; the place where this action occurs

interlocking–an interconnection of signals and signal appliances such that their movements must succeed each other in a predetermined sequence, ensuring that signals cannot be displayed simultaneously on conflicting routes.

jitney–taxicab

jointed rail–sectioned rail, joined together by bolts and joint bars; also called bolted rail (see welded rail; low joint)

journal box–the housing surrounding a journal or friction bearing containing oil-soaked packing known as waste (see friction bearing)

juice–electricity, especially if delivered by overhead catenary (see catenary)

kicker–see dynamiter

kiss–to collide

knock down–the actuation of a signal by a train

knuckle–the pivoting part of a coupler that swings closed upon coupling to interlock with a knuckle on another coupler; must be in the open position for coupling to take place (see coupler; drawbar; draft gear)

ladder–main track leading into a yard from which yard tracks diverge (see lead; turnout)

layover–time spent waiting for another train

lead–main track from which others diverge (see ladder; turnout)

lead unit–the first locomotive unit in a train consist

leasers–locomotives leased from leasing companies or other railroads to help overcome motive power shortages; also called rent-a-wrecks

left-hand side–side of the locomotive cab occupied by the conductor or assistant engineer (see right-hand side)

level crossing–Canadian term for grade crossing

limited speed–for passenger trains, speed not exceeding 45 mph; for freights, speed not exceeding 40 mph

limo–taxicab

line–a rail line; to align track switches to set up a particular route (see switch)

lineup–the order in which trains are to traverse a rail line

loading–the ability of a locomotive to exert tractive force in a train

loads–loaded rail cars (see empties)

local–a freight train that switches industries within a set boundary, usually within a distance that allows the train and crew to return to the terminal of departure before outlawing; also called a wayfreight or shifter (see turn; outlaw)

low joint–in jointed-rail trackage, a joint that has loosened, allowing the track to sag when bearing loads (see jointed rail)

lubricators–devices that lubricate car and locomotive wheel flanges to reduce wheel and track wear, especially on curves; normally mounted on locomotives or track structures

lunch bucket–large, lunchbox-shaped portable radios typically carried with a shoulder strap

MK–railcars and locomotives manufactured by Morrison-Knudsen

MLW–a locomotive manufactured by the Montreal Locomotive Works

MU–abbreviation for multiple-unit operation, whereby a single locomotive, usually in the lead, controls the operation of multiple locomotives in a consist; an electrically powered passenger train consisting of one or more powered cars with or without unpowered trailers

maintenance-of-way (MOW)–the term for the persons and activities associated with maintaining the fixed structures and trackage necessary to move trains over a railroad

manifest–see hotshot

marker–a reflector, flag, light, or other highly visible marking device in the red-orange-amber color range that is affixed to the rear of a train to indicate that the train is complete (see blinker, EOT)

mast–a signal support consisting of a single support base and associated signal-mounting hardware (see dwarf)

medium speed–speed not exceeding 30 mph

merchandise–goods and materials carried in a train

merry-go-round–turntable

motor–an electric locomotive

movement–any train traversing any trackage in a rail network

naught–zero

normal speed–the maximum authorized speed

notch–throttle positions in a locomotive, typically numbered from 1 (slowest) to 8 (fastest); also called run

notch out–to accelerate a locomotive; also called widen on it (see notch)

number boards–the illuminated panels on the front, sides, or back of a locomotive that display the unit number of the locomotive

OS–on-sheet; used to report a train to a dispatcher

office train–see executive train

oil can–tank car containing fuel oil

on the advertised–according to schedule; on time

on the ground–any personnel on the right-of-way not on board a locomotive or train; derailment

on the pin–zero car lengths distance (see car lengths)

operator–person responsible for relaying train orders to train crews and operating switches and signals under the direction of a dispatcher (see dispatcher)

orders–short for train orders; instructions for the operation of a train (see Forms)

outlaw–a member of a train crew that has exceeded the Federally mandated hours-of-service limits; to do so (see hours-of-service law)

pantograph–the device that collects electrical current from an overhead catenary to power an electric locomotive or locomotives (see catenary)

passing track–a siding that allows one train meet or pass another (see siding)

pickup–to retrieve cars from interchanges and sidings; a pantograph (see interchange; drop off; siding; pantograph)

piggyback–the transport of highway trailers on flatcars; also called TOFC

pigs–piggybacked trailers

pilot–an employee assigned to a train or track car when the engineer, conductor, or track car driver is not qualified on the physical characteristics or the operating rules of the territory to be traversed; the front part of a locomotive below the nose or walkway used to clear obstructions from tracks, sometimes used as a snowplow

plant–any fixed object on a railroad; short for interlocking plant (see interlocking)

plow–snowplow (see pilot; spreader; rotary)

polling–an illegal method of moving cars on adjacent tracks wherein a pushpole is placed between the cars to be moved and a locomotive on an adjacent track; unlikely to be discussed on the radio

private varnish–passenger cars owned by private individuals; usually coupled onto the end of regular passenger trains

protection–any action or device, such as grade crossing signals, necessary for the continued safe operation of trains in a rail network (see flag; torpedoes)

pull the pin—to uncouple a car

puller—train that transfers cars from yard to yard; see transfer

push-pull operation—a method of operating a train whereby locomotives are not switched to the head end when the train changes direction; typically a control car is used on the end opposite the engine to facilitate push moves; used almost exclusively in commuter operations (see run-around)

pusher—a type of helper locomotive added to the end of a train consist (see helper)

RIP tracks—abbreviation for repair-in-place tracks; tracks where simple repairs are made to cars and locomotives

RTC—abbreviation for rail traffic controller (see dispatcher)

racetrack—a long, straight, high-speed stretch of railroad

rail grinder—a maintenance train that restores the proper profile to a railhead through grinding and abrading; also called a grinder

rail traffic controller—see dispatcher

reduction—a brake application

reefer—an insulated boxcar containing a mechanical refrigeration unit; used for transporting perishable goods, particularly fruits and vegetables

reporting marks—code letters stenciled on the sides and ends of freight cars to indicate car ownership; used in conjunction with car numbers (see car numbers)

restricted speed—a speed that allows a train to stop within one-half the range of vision, short of a train, obstruction, improperly lined switch, or broken rail; speed must not exceed 20 mph outside interlocking limits or 15 mph within interlocking limits; speed applies to the entire movement

restriction—an order limiting or otherwise restricting the operation of a train (see order)

retainers—valves that hold air brake pressure on a car; usually are set before descending steep or long grades to facilitate train braking

ribbon rail—see welded rail

rip-rap–boulders, scrapped railroad cars, or other heavy objects placed along roadbeds to prevent erosion from flooding

right-hand side–the engineer's side of a locomotive cab (see left-hand side)

roadswitcher–a hood-unit freight locomotive suited for use on mainlines and in yards; the hood design offers good visibility and collision protection (see switcher; hood unit)

rockers–vandals and trespassers who throw rocks or other objects at trains, especially locomotives and cabooses (see vandals; trespassers; ghetto grates)

rotary–a type of snowplow that uses rotating blades to throw snow clear of the right-of-way (see spreader)

Rule 93–rule governing movements within yard limits; normally, trains must operate at restricted speed

Rule G–operating rule forbidding the influence, possession, or use of alcohol and other intoxicants by railroad personnel while on duty

ruling grade–the grade on a line that results in maximum limitation to train operations

run–the train to which a crew is assigned; a throttle setting (see notch)

run 8–full throttle, also called notch 8 (see notch)

runaround–a method of reversing train direction by moving locomotives from one end of a train to the other through the use of crossovers and an adjacent track; the tracks used to perform a runaround; a long air hose used to bypass a car with a defective brake system (see crossover; push-pull operation; train line)

running light–locomotives running alone or in MU without railcars

running track–a track on which movements may be made by signal indication or at restricted speed under the direction of an employee designated in the timetable

runthrough–an operation in which locomotives and cars move from the tracks of one railroad to another without stopping to change locomotives and, on occasion, crews; a train performing runthrough operations

Glossary of Terms • 187

SD—an abbreviation and model prefix for "special duty," a general term for six-axle, hood-type, roadswitching locomotives manufactured by Electro-Motive or General Motors (see hood unit; roadswitcher)

safety cab—a locomotive cab with a full-width nose and a desktop control console (see desktop control; Canadian cab)

sander—a device on a locomotive that applies sand to the railhead immediately before the wheels to improve traction (see grit; slip)

schedule—the part of a timetable that prescribes direction, number, frequency, and times for movement of designated trains

scheduled train—a train designated by timetable schedule (see extra)

service application—any brake application other than an emergency application

set out—to place cars into sidings or spurs, often used when referring to removing bad order cars from a consist (see bad order)

shifter—see local

shoofly—temporary trackage laid around construction sites, flooded areas, derailments, etc.

short-time crew—crew approaching the limit of the hours-of-service law (see hours-of-service law; outlaw)

shed—a small engine house; a snowshed (see snowshed)

siding—a side track used to park or store cars or to allow one train to meet or pass another (see passing track; stub track)

slide fence—a fence consisting of electrical conductors erected in areas along tracks subject to frequent rockslides; when broken by falling rocks, the loss of conduction activates signals to indicate the presence of obstructions on the tracks

slip—loss of traction by a locomotive; also called wheelslip (see sander)

slow speed—speed not exceeding 15 mph

slug—a locomotive that consists only of traction motors and ballast; electrical power for the motors is obtained from an adjacent "mother" locomotive

snow melter–an on-track device that melts ice and snow on remote-controlled switches to help ensure reliable operation in cold weather; usually electric or gas powered; usually operated by a dispatcher; also called a switch heater or heater

snow shed–a wooden enclosure placed over and around tracks to protect trains from drifting and avalanching

special move–any movement requiring special handling such as an oversized or heavy load or a military hardware shipment

speeder–a small, gasoline-powered maintenance vehicle typically used by track inspectors in Canada (see track car)

spiked switch–a switch that has been temporarily or permanently lined in one direction with track spikes

spill–accidental discharge of car contents; derailment

spot–to place a car in a designated position

spreader–a plow-type maintenance vehicle used for snow-clearing and ballast-spreading activities

sprint–time-sensitive freight train; (see hotshot)

spur–a short stretch of track diverging from a main or branchline to serve a customer located away from the primary trackage (see branch)

stabbed–to be routed into and stopped in a passing track by a dispatcher; also called stabbed, cooling your heels

stack train–a train consisting of double-stack containers in well cars (see double-stack; filet; well car)

stacks–see double-stack

stem–any rail line

streak of rust–a little-used or abandoned rail line

stretching the slack–an action by a locomotive engineer wherein the space between cars, or slack, is slowly increased to avoid jerking cars into motion (see bunching the slack)

stub track–a siding that deadends without rejoining the main track

switch–a device that allows trains to move from one track to another by diverting or guiding the train wheels as they move through a switch; operated locally by manual action or remotely using electric motors; to move cars from one track to another or drop off and pick up cars

switch list–car placement instructions used by yard crews to assemble blocks of cars (see block)

switcher–a small locomotive used in yard and switching operations; similar to a roadswitcher, but lacking a short hood (see roadswitcher)

TOFC–abbreviation for trailer-on-flatcar; also called piggyback (see COFC)

team track–a siding or stub track used to place cars for loading and unloading by firms lacking a dedicated siding; named for the horses formerly used to haul goods to and from the siding (see siding; stub track)

test train–a special movement for the purpose of testing new operations or equipment

tie up–to park a train or locomotive for an extended period of time for crew changes or breaks

timetable–a schedule for governing train movements and operations

tissues–see flimsies

torch–to scrap railcars or locomotives

torpedo–an explosive signalling device, placed on the railhead and detonated by a passing locomotive

tower–a control center in a yard or along a main line used to direct and regulate train movements

track car–a maintenance vehicle, typically a standard over-the-road vehicle modified with retractable railroad wheels, used by track inspectors for on-track inspections; also called hi-rail

track circuit–a circuit that uses the rails as conductors, when shorted by train axles, activates crossing signals, lineside signals, etc.

track speed–the speed limit for a track or stretch of track

track warrant–see Form D

trackmobile–a rubber-tired locomotive with retractable rail wheels for use both on and off the rails

train line–train air brake line, used to control train braking by increasing or decreasing air pressure; decreases in pressure result in increased braking (see air hose)

transfer–a train that moves cars between rail yards

trespasser–any unauthorized person on railroad property (see vandal; daisy picker; foamer)

trick–shift of duty

trim–to reswitch errant cars in a hump yard

trimmer–switch engine performing trim moves

truck–the wheelset and associated supporting hardware under cars and locomotives

turn–short for turnaround, a local that leaves a terminal and makes a round trip within hours-of-service limits without a crew change (see local)

turnout–a switch and its associated trackage diverting from a rail line (see crossover; switch)

turntable–a rotating section of track used to turn locomotives, end for end, to facilitate reversals in train direction

u-boats–general term for locomotives manufactured by General Electric. especially older models

unit train–a dedicated train carrying a single commodity, such as coal, bound for a specific customer

van–caboose; also called hack, buggy, cabin

vandals–trespassers bent on defacing or destroying railroad property (see rockers; trespassers)

war zone–any dangerous area, typically in inner cities; with high rates of violence and crime that threaten the safety and security of train crews, operations, and lading

walkway–the area inside cab units and along both sides of the long hood on hood units, used by locomotive crews to walk from unit-to-unit when trains are in motion

wash racks–the area in a locomotive servicing facility used to clean the outside of locomotives

waste–see journal box

wayfreight–see local

weed sprayer–a maintenance vehicle that applies weed-control herbicides to the right-of-way

weld–used to join severed sections of welded rail; sometimes performed in the field using thermal-powder welding kits (see welded rail)

welded rail–short for continuous welded rail; rail sections that have been welded together, end to end, to form a long, continuous stretch of rail; also called ribbon rail (see jointed rail; weld)

wells–short for well cars, cars with deep pockets into which double-stacked containers are placed (see double stacks)

wheel slip–see slip

widen on it–see notch out

wipe the clock–to stop a train as a result of an emergency brake application; also called wipe the gauge; big hole (see emergency braking)

wye–a track structure used to reverse the direction a train, wherein a train traverses a triangular- or Y-shaped section of track; first, the train heads into one leg of the wye, backs across the top, and then heads out in the opposite direction on the other leg (see balloon track)

yard limits–the main track area between Yard Limit signs as designated in the timetable; movements within yard limits are governed by Rule 93 (see Rule 93)

12dB SINAD 78, 79
20dB quieting 78

AAR channels 29, 30, 82
AEI 51, 53
ARRL 122, 125
ATC 141, 142
ac mains 74, 86, 116, 120
accidents 63
adaptors 89, 133
advance warning 68
Aerotron 17
Alton Route 15
amplifier
    audio 114-116
    gain 109
    noise 109
    signal 103, 105-109, 119, 120
    testing 108, 109
amplitude modulation (AM) 20
Amtech Corp. 141
antennas
    active 108
    adjustable whip 90, 93
    attic 99
    base/repeater 23, 26, 27, 99-102
    beam 117, 118
    built-in 38
    citizen's band 123
    directional 19, 23
    firecracker 37
    gain 19, 118
    glass mount 95, 97
    ground plane 123
    grounding 101, 102
    gutter mount 95
    ham 123
    half-wave dipole 133-138
    hardware 99, 122
    hole mount 95
    homebuilt 130-138
    installation 131, 137, 138
    insulators 134
    loading coils 91
    low profile 37
    magnetic mount 97, 98
    marine 99
    mobile 94-99
    outdoor 99-102
    radome 37
    rotors 118
    rubber duckies 90, 93
    SO-239 130-133
    safety 94, 100, 102, 119
    television 124
    towers 119
    trunk lip mount 94, 95
    tuning 91, 92, 99, 123
    used 123-125
    whip 37
    window mount 94
    zoning 119, 120
Atlantic Coast Line 8
Auburn, Wash. 13
Automatic Electric Co. 17
automotive electricals 86
Aviation Accessories Corp. 8

BART 141
BC Transit 11
ballast 53, 54, 62
Baltimore & Ohio 11, 12
base stations 23, 26, 31, 37
batteries 16, 74, 85, 86
Bendix 13
Bessemer & Lake Erie 8
Binghamton, N.Y. 12
blind spots 41
blocks 3
bowl 59, 60
bowlmaster 59
brakeman 15, 55
Brown, A.C. 6
bungalow 23, 45
Burlington Northern Santa Fe 141
Burlington Route 12, 13
burst transmission 48

CP Rail 141
CTC 57
CTCSS (see coded squelch)
cables 86
cabooses 12, 13, 16, 30, 38, 41, 57
Canadian National 12, 141
Carryphone 11
cellular telephone 46, 141, 142
Champion 11

channel banks 82-85
chargers 85
Chesapeake & Ohio 11
Chicago, Ill. 12
citizen's band (CB) 18, 20, 121
Clyde, Ill. 13
coaxial cable (see feedline)
coaxial switch 101, 104
coded squelch 29, 37, 46, 112-114
coded squelch decoders 112, 113
coils, track 7
computer databases 142
computer interfaces 110, 112
conductor 6, 16
connectors
    BNC 104, 133
    PL-259 104, 133
    SO-239 130-133
Conrail 79, 80
current draw 38, 86, 87

DTMF (see Touch Tones)
data communications 17, 48, 143
DeForest Wireless Co. 8, 12
delay 84, 110
derailments 63
digital communications 143
dispatcher 3, 6, 14, 21-31, 58, 61, 63
dispatching center 21
divulgence 67
doubling 30
Dunbar, W.K. 15
duplexer 27

ECPA 67, 143
EOT 41, 43, 69, 70
e-mail 143
Easton, Pa. 7
Edison, Thomas 7, 8
Electro-Motive 141
engineers 43, 55
Erie Railroad 13
external speakers 114-116

FAA 120
FCC 18, 64, 139
fax 143
feedline
    loss 102, 103, 105, 108, 119

routing 103
used 122, 123, 125
flagman 6, 15
flea markets 121
frequency
    EOT 43
    allocations 17
    counters 82, 83
    guides 81
    ham 72
    hopping 50
    repeater 27
    room monitor 117
frequency modulation (FM) 8
fusee 3

GMRS 18
General Electric 8, 12, 17, 141
General Railway Signal 8, 141
generators 16
global positioning (GPS) 50
Godfrey, Ill. 15
Great Northern Railway 13
ground planes 92, 94, 99
Gulf, Mobile & Ohio 12, 15

ham radio 14, 72, 121
ham radio equipment 110
hamfests 121
hand signals 55
Harmon 141
Harris Corp. 17, 141
headphones 115
hog law 64
homebrewing 129-138
hooping up 3
Hughes 141
hump 13, 59
hump conductor 59
humpmaster 59
hybrids 15

identifying trains 70
inductive systems 6-11
Industry Canada 18, 64, 139
instruction manuals 81
interference 105, 110
interference filters 105

intermodulation 80, 105

Jersey Central 11

Kansas City Southern 11

Lackawanna Route 12
leaky cables 26
Lehigh Valley Railroad 7
lightning 101, 102
line-of-sight transmission 18, 99
lockout 83, 84, 110
locomotives 12, 13, 30, 37
locomotives, helper 53, 54, 58
logger 114
loudspeakers 74, 77, 116
lunch buckets 38

MTA 141
maintenance forces 21, 26, 27, 54, 61
Marconi Wireless Co. 12
maritime radio 139
matching transformer 124
Mexico 17
microphones 38
microwave 17-23, 26, 66
Milwaukee Road 7, 11
Minnesota Iron Range 13
mobile radios 30, 31
Motorola 17
multicouplers 98, 104
multiple unit operation (MU) 53
Municipal Railway 11

narrowband FM 20
National Electric Code 101
National Weather Service 129
Nellybelle 13, 14
New Castle, Pa. 12
New York, N.Y. 12
New York Central 8, 11, 12
nimbies 120
non-voice transmissions 66
Norfolk & Western 10, 11, 13
Norfolk Southern 43
Northern Pacific 13

Omaha, Nebr. 11, 12
open wire lines 13, 17, 48, 63

operators 3, 6, 69
Order of Railway Telegraphers 14
overloading 105

PBX 46-48, 61, 84
paging systems 80
Pennsylvania Railroad 8-11, 12
Perth Junction, N.J. 7
pin puller 59
polarization 124, 133
police 21, 26, 63
portable radios 37, 38
power lines 94, 100, 101
power sources 85, 86
priority 84
Private Line™ 29
professional equipment 109, 110, 118
propagation 19
pull down 59
pull moves 59

RAD 43, 44, 57, 69, 70, 114
RCA 12
radio, introduction of 11
Radio Amateur's Handbook 125
railfans 65, 68, 72, 81
railfanning 68-72
railroad network 1
receivers 16, 20, 26, 110
recorders 112, 113
remote control 13, 53-56, 153-156
remote receivers 38
regulation, government 12
repeaters
    active 26
    area 116, 117
    local 27, 37
    passive 26, 120
    remote control 56
retarders 59
roadmasters 61
Rochester & Southern 79, 80
Rockwell 141
room monitors 116
rulebook 14
runthrough operation 18

SHF radio 18-20
San Francisco, Calif. 11

Index • 195

satellite 48
scan cycles 84
scanners
    base 74
    buying 72, 73
    crystal 123, 125, 128
    definition 65
    dynamic range 80
    legality 66
    mobile 67, 77
    operation 81-87
    performance 77
    portable 74
    selectivity 79, 80
    sensitivity 77, 78, 105, 108
    stands 93
    used 125, 128
Scranton, Pa. 12
Seattle, Wash. 13
semi-duplex operation 27, 47
service monitors 110, 125
shortlines 23, 27, 54, 65
signal amplifiers 103, 105-109, 120
signals 21
simplex operation 29, 30
Smith, Willoughby 7
soldering 129, 130
solid state 15
Southern Pacific Lines 141
spectrum congestion 139
spread spectrum 50
squelch 15, 66
Staten Island, N.Y. 7
static charge 102
Stromberg Carlson 17
superintendent 3
switches, track 21

taxis 64
telegraph 6, 7
telemetry 17, 48, 70, 142
theft 63, 71, 98
Touch Tones™ 31
train
    orders 3
    schedules 2
    symbols 70, 71
trainmasters 61

Trainphone 8, 11
transformers 86, 87
transmitter ID 64
transmitters 16, 20, 23, 26
Transport Canada 120
trespassing 63, 71
trim moves 13, 59
trunked radio 139-142
trunking tones 143
tuners 128, 129

UHF radio 17-20, 51
Union Pacific 11, 70, 141
Union Switch & Signal 8, 141
unions 14
used gear 121-129

VHF radio
    introduction of 11, 12
    frequencies 17, 18
    propagation 19, 20
vacuum tubes 15
Vancouver, B.C. 11
vandalism 63, 71, 98
Vibroplex 17
voice communications 17, 66
voting 41, 140

Western Electric Co. 12
Westinghouse 8, 12
wideband FM 20
wireless microphones 117
World War II 8, 12
wreckmasters 61

Y-adapter 116
Yakima, Wash. 13
yard operations 58, 59
yardmasters 61

Zenith 12
Zephyr 12

About the Author

Vincent Reh was born in Rome, N.Y. in 1960 and has held a lifelong interest in railroads and radio. He spent his early years in Verona and Greenway, small towns along the celebrated New York Central Water Level Route, where he witnessed the evolution of the Central into Conrail. He later lived in Utica, Rochester, and Batavia, N.Y. and Ft. Lauderdale, Fla., usually managing to locate within sight of a main line.

Mr. Reh holds a B.T. in Electrical Engineering and an M.A. in Communication from the State University of New York. He is a 21-year radio ham and holds advanced class call WA2AUY. He has worked as a technician, engineer, technical writer, and marketing copywriter with Motorola, Inc. and Harris Corporation. He is also a member of the New York Museum of Transportation, the Empire State Passenger Association, Morse Telegraph Club, Radio Amateurs of Northern Vermont, and the Society for Technical Communication.

Currently residing on Grand Isle, Vt. with his wife Louise and the ghost of the Rutland, Mr. Reh works as a freelance writer and continues to pursue other interests including photography, local history, interurban railways, Cajun French culture, ice hockey, tube amplifiers, old electric guitars and basses, and his '68 Ford Falcon.

Additional copies of this book are available direct from the publisher for $19.95 plus $3.50 shipping ($5.50 shipping for addresses outside North America). Vermont residents must add $1.00 sales tax. Please mail check or money order, in U.S. funds, to the address below.

To comment on this book or to find out about other titles available from the publisher, please write:

Byron Hill Publishing Co.
P.O. Box 197
Grand Isle, Vt. 05458

or dial (802) 372-6557

Dealer enquiries invited; quantity discounts available.